The Human Right to Water

Law, Justice, and Development

The Law, Justice, and Development series is offered by the Legal Vice Presidency of the World Bank to provide insights into aspects of law and justice that are relevant to the development process. Works in the series present new legal and judicial reform activities related to the World Bank's work, as well as analyses of domestic and international law. The series is intended to be accessible to a broad audience as well as to legal practitioners.

Series editors: David Freestone and Salman M. A. Salman

The Human Right to Water

Legal and Policy Dimensions

Salman M. A. Salman
Lead Counsel
Environmentally and Socially Sustainable Development and
International Law Group
Legal Vice Presidency
The World Bank

Siobhán McInerney-Lankford
Counsel
Environmentally and Socially Sustainable Development and
International Law Group
Legal Vice Presidency
The World Bank

THE WORLD BANK
Washington, D.C.

0-8213-5922-3

Library of Congress Cataloging-in-Publication Data
Salman, Salman M. A., 1948-
   The human right to water : legal and policy dimensions / Salman M.A. Salman, Siobhán McInerney-Lankford.
     p. cm. — (Law, justice, and development)
   Includes bibliographical references and index.
   ISBN 0-8213-5922-3
     1. Water rights. 2. Human rights. I. McInerney-Lankford, Siobhán Alice, 1974-
  II. Title. III. Series.

   K3260.S25 2004
   341.4'8—dc22

                       2004054887

Contents

Foreword

Human rights and water resources are among the most compelling issues to have captured the attention of the world community in recent years. As a result, these topics have been placed at the top of the global development agenda, occupying a prominent place at conferences and forums and generating debate that has been both extensive and complex.

The nexus among development, water, and human rights has long been recognized. In 1992, the Dublin Conference on "Water and Development" and the Rio Summit on "Environment and Development" recognized, *inter alia,* the basic right of all human beings to have access to clean water and sanitation and acknowledged this right as a "commonly agreed premise." Shortly thereafter, the World Conference on Human Rights held in Vienna, Austria, in 1993, confirmed that all human rights—economic, social, cultural, political, and civil—are universal, indivisible, interdependent, and interrelated. It also affirmed that extreme poverty constitutes a violation of human dignity and called for urgent steps to be taken to achieve a better understanding of poverty and its causes. The linkage between poverty and water shortage is well established—poverty is prevalent mostly in water-short areas. The majority of those who do not have sufficient drinking water (more than one billion people), and those who have no provision for sanitation (more than two billion people), are in the poorer areas of the developing world.

Thus, a gradual recognition of the centrality of water to the realization of the rights enshrined in the Universal Declaration of Human Rights, as well as in the International Covenant on Economic, Social and Cultural Rights, and the Declaration on the Right to Development, has begun to emerge. This was confirmed some 10 years after Dublin, Rio, and Vienna, in General Comment No. 15, issued by the Committee on Economic, Social and Cultural Rights in 2002. The Comment set forth, in unequivocal terms, the direct relationship between human rights and water, and provided explicit recognition of the human right to water itself.

Accordingly, this Study, which considers the human right to water from legal and policy perspectives, comes at an opportune time and should help clarify the significance of the debate on the human right to water and its relevance to development. The Legal Vice Presidency is pleased to offer this publication and hopes it will serve as a useful reference for all those concerned with human rights and water resources.

Roberto Dañino
Senior Vice President and General Counsel
The World Bank

July 30, 2004

Abstract

The evolution of the right to water can be traced to the developments of the early 1970s. This Study analyzes the resolutions and declarations of the various conferences and forums that have been held since that time, and the ways in which they have confronted the issue of the right to water. The Study then discusses the evolution of the international legal regime for the protection and promotion of human rights, and pays particular attention to the Universal Declaration of Human Rights and the International Covenant on Economic, Social and Cultural Rights, as well as to the International Covenant on Civil and Political Rights. The role of each of the committees established to oversee the implementation of the two Covenants is considered in some detail. Particular attention is given to the Committee on Economic, Social and Cultural Rights, its evolution, and its strengthening, and the practice of issuing General Comments. The last two parts of the Study are devoted to General Comment No. 15, which recognizes the human right to water. These parts analyze the extent to which the Comment recognizes a legal right to water, and highlights some policy aspects that are related to, and may affect, this right. The core thesis of this book is that there exists, within the legal framework of the International Covenant on Economic, Social and Cultural Rights, a human right to water because it is a right that inheres in several other rights, and a right without which key provisions of the Covenant would be rendered ineffectual. This conclusion is buttressed also by the interpretative authority that lies with the Committee having evolved from its initial form as a Working Group, to what is now undeniably, a fully-fledged entity, with significant formal authority and legitimacy. Although this conclusion acknowledges that General Comments do not create *new rights*, it recognizes that General Comment No. 15 extrapolates the normative and practical bases of a human right to water within the fabric of the International Covenant on Economic, Social and Cultural Rights. Together with a number of General Assembly resolutions on the issue, including the Millennium Development Goal related to water, as well as the voluminous body of soft law provisions, the General Comment arguably provides further evidence that there is an incipient right to water evolving in public international law today. Moreover, the Comment has offered a new momentum to efforts aimed at translating those soft law commitments into substantive, precise, and legally binding obligations.

Acknowledgments

We would like to extend our thanks and appreciation to Daniel Bradlow, David Freestone, Mohan Gopal, Alfredo Sfeir-Younis, and Kishor Uprety for valuable comments on earlier drafts of this book. Our thanks are also due to Roberto Dañino, Senior Vice President and General Counsel, for encouraging us to expand the scope of the original paper into the current manuscript, and for his unwavering support of this project. We would also like to thank our colleagues in the Law Resource Center of the World Bank, Linda Thompson, Laura Lalime-Mowry, Wendy Melis, and Martha Weiss, for their support with materials for the research for this book. Our thanks are also due to Mary May Agcaoili, Lakshmi Mathew, and Ferozan Hashimi for assistance in various ways in the preparation of this book, and to Shéhan de Sayrah for his editorial assistance.

Abbreviations

ECOSOC	Economic and Social Council (of the United Nations)
GWP	Global Water Partnership
ICCPR	International Covenant on Civil and Political Rights
ICESCR	International Covenant on Economic, Social and Cultural Rights
ICSID	International Centre for Settlement of Investment Disputes
ILC	International Law Commission of the United Nations
NGO	Non-governmental Organization
OHCHR	Office of the High Commissioner for Human Rights
Res	Resolution of the United Nations General Assembly
U.N.	United Nations
UDHR	Universal Declaration of Human Rights
UNCED	United Nations Conference on Environment and Development
UN/ECE	United Nations Economic Commission for Europe
UNGA	United Nations General Assembly
UNICEF	United Nations Children's Fund
WCD	World Commission on Dams
WCW	World Commission for Water in the 21st Century
WHO	World Health Organization
WWC	World Water Council

INTRODUCTION

Water is an indispensable element for life. Social and economic development is closely tied to water. Poverty is prevalent mostly in areas that face water shortage. Water-related diseases, caused by unsafe drinking water and the absence of proper sanitation facilities, are among the leading causes of death in the developing world. The fact that the world faces a water crisis is obvious. It is reported that more than 2 billion people are affected by water shortages in over 40 countries, 1.1 billion people do not have sufficient drinking water, and 2.4 billion people have no provision for sanitation. Current predictions forecast that by 2050 at least one in four people is likely to live in a country affected by chronic or recurring shortages of fresh water.[1] One reason for this crisis is hydrological variability in most parts of the world. Another major contributing factor is the overwhelming increase in population and urbanization, and the resulting environmental degradation. The world population has more than tripled during the last century, while water uses for human purposes have multiplied sixfold.[2] With the continued upsurge in population growth, and with the finite amount of water, this situation is sure to worsen. It will, in turn, sharpen the competing demands of the different uses and users for the finite amount of water that is available. Under these circumstances, questions are being raised regarding the relative priority of the different water uses, how to protect those uses, and how to guarantee access of the poor and the vulnerable groups to sufficient quantities of water. The foregoing has gradually led the global debate to focus on the human right to water, which now occupies a prominent place on the agenda of the international water community.

"Human Rights is the idea of our time."[3] These are the prophetic words of Louis Henkin, and what he asserts is undoubtedly true. However, defining human rights remains notoriously difficult. Basic definitions assert that "every human

---

[1] *Water for People, Water for Life: The United Nations World Water Development Report,* (World Water Assessment Program), 10 (UNESCO Publishing 2003).

[2] William J. Cosgrove & Frank R. Rijsberman, *World Water Vision—Making Water Everybody's Business* (World Water Council), 4 (Earthscan Publications Ltd. 2000).

[3] Louis Henkin, *Introduction* in *The International Bill of Rights* (Louis Henkin, ed., Columbia University Press 1981).

being, in every society, is entitled to have basic autonomy and freedoms respected and basic needs satisfied."[4] Jack Donnelly offered the following definition: "human rights, droits de l'homme, derechos humanos, Menscherechte, 'the rights of man' are literally the rights that one has because one is human."[5] Maurice Cranston defines a human right as "a universal moral right, something which all men everywhere, at all times ought to have, something of which no one may be deprived without a grave affront to justice, something which is owing to every human being simply because he is human."[6] In a similar vein, Laurie Wiseberg opines, "Human rights are entitlements due to every man, woman, and child because they are human . . . They are nonderogable rights: Their violation can never be justified, even by a state of national emergency."[7] After enumerating the different categories of the civil, political, economic, social, and cultural rights, Wiseberg concludes, "The premise of current international law is that these rights are inherent in the human person: They are not *given* to people by the State, and the State cannot deprive people of their rights."[8] Unfortunately, the gap between those noble ideals and the reality of substantive commitments and entitlements has remained quite wide. Gross violations of human rights—economic, social, cultural, civil, and political—are widespread, even in countries that are parties to international human rights treaties. State sovereignty has often been posited as existing in conflict with human rights, and has been mobilized in defense of a state's prerogative not to provide meaningful protection to such rights, or to supersede the obligations to implement human rights instruments.[9] As Steiner and Alston observe:

> At its very threshold and to this day, the human rights movement has inevitably confronted antagonistic claims based on conceptions of sov-

---

[4] *See id.*

[5] Jack Donnelly, *Universal Human Rights in Theory and Practice*, 7 (2d ed., Cornell University Press 2003). *See also* Jack Donnelly, *International Human Rights*, 19 (Westview Press 1993).

[6] Maurice Cranston, *What are Human Rights*, 36 (Taplinger Publishing Co. 1973). *See also* Jack Donnelly, *The Concept of Human Rights*, (Croom Helm 1985).

[7] Laurie S. Wiseberg, *Introductory Essay*, in Edward Lawson, *Encyclopedia of Human Rights*, xix (2d ed., Taylor and Francis 1996).

[8] *See id.*

[9] For an excellent collection of pieces considering various aspects of sovereignty, *see The Transformation of Sovereignty* in *Proceedings of the Eighty-Eighth Annual Meeting, the American Society of International Law*, Washington D.C. (1994).

ereignty. How could its premises coexist with the then reigning concepts of state sovereignty? Or have the nature of the state, and the content of that protean concept as well as of allied concepts like domestic jurisdiction and autonomy, themselves undergone substantial change over the half century of this movement?[10]

What cannot be doubted is that the relational position of human rights and sovereignty has undergone some significant changes, and that the distinction between matters that are within exclusive domestic purview, and those that are legitimately within the remit of the international community's concerns, is no longer a stark one.[11] Moreover, the slow but steady growth in the global recognition of human rights and their relevance to an ever-increasing number of areas that were hitherto considered unrelated to human rights, should encourage a belief that the adherence to human rights standards, and the increase in their substantive implementation, will also grow. The work and commitment of the United Nations agencies to fulfill their mandates under the various human rights instruments must be lauded for giving increased visibility and legitimacy to the human rights they cover, and ultimately, to furthering their realization. The steady work of those agencies is both supported by the shifting relationship described above, and evidence of it. These are encouraging developments, but they are also essential to ensuring the realization of human rights generally, and the human right to water in particular.

As indicated above, the definition of any human right presents a daunting task, but the difficulty of defining a human right to water is compounded by the fact that water is both a vital and a minimum need, and therefore indispensable to human life. Denying people water is to deny them the right to life. Despite that, the current thinking is that water should not be viewed only as a social good and a human need, but also as a commodity, the economic value of which must be recognized so as to manage demand, and avoid wasteful and environmentally damaging uses. Striking a balance between the two considerations, particularly in

---

[10] Henry J. Steiner & Philip Alston, *International Human Rights in Context: Law, Politics and Morals,* 573 (2d ed., Clarendon Press 2000).

[11] *See* Louis Goodman, *Democracy, Sovereignty and Intervention,* 9(1) Am. U. J of Int'l Law and Policy 27 (1993). *See also* Louis Henkin, *The Rights of Man Today*, 94 (Westview Press 1978). Discussing the U.N. Charter, Henkin holds "the new law buried the old dogma that the individual is not a subject of international law and that a government's behavior toward its own national is a matter of domestic not international concern. It penetrated national frontiers and the veil of sovereignty."

light of the expanding role of the private sector in water resources management on the one hand, and the increasing recognition of the rights of the poor and vulnerable groups to water on the other, presents a major challenge. It is in this context that the concept of the human right to water has acquired more relevance and meaning. Fortunately, some innovative approaches for addressing this difficulty have started to emerge gradually around the world.

This Study aims at discussing and analyzing the concept of the human right to water. As such, the Study deals both with human rights and water, and attempts to explain the linkages between the two. The Study begins with a review of the resolutions and declarations of the various conferences and forums on the notion of water as a basic human need, as well as the right to water. The Study then discusses the evolution of the international legal regime for human rights, paying particular attention to the International Bill of Human Rights.[12] After an overview of the provisions of the Universal Declaration of Human Rights (UDHR) and its status under contemporary international human rights law, the Study analyzes the two human rights Covenants: the International Covenant on Economic, Social and Cultural Rights (ICESCR), and the International Covenant on Civil and Political Rights (ICCPR). Particular attention is paid to the institutional mechanism for each of the two Covenants. Whereas the Human Rights Committee is a treaty entity established explicitly under the ICCPR, no such mechanism is provided for under the ICESCR. This necessitates a thorough analysis of the evolution of the institutional mechanism for overseeing the implementation of the ICESCR from a working group into the gradual expansion of the role and responsibilities of the Committee on Economic, Social and Cultural Rights, and the jurisprudential value of the General Comments it has issued. This sets the stage for a thorough analysis of General Comment No. 15 on the right to water, the basis for the recognition of this right, its legal and policy dimensions, as well as the implications that ensue.

International water conferences and forums have vacillated between declaring water a basic human need on the one hand, and a right on the other. As will

---

[12] The International Bill of Human Rights is the collective term for the Universal Declaration of Human Rights; the International Covenant on Economic, Social and Cultural Rights; and the International Covenant on Civil and Political Rights and its two Optional Protocols; *see* Fact Sheet No. 2 (Rev. 1) at <http://www.unhchr.ch/html/menu6/2/fs2.htm>.

be discussed later, the Mar del Plata Water Conference of 1977 stated that all people have the right to have access to water in quantities and of a quality equal to their basic needs. However, 15 years later, the Rio Conference emphasized that priority has to be given to the satisfaction of basic needs, and made no direct reference to the issue of a right to water. Similarly, the three World Water Forums that were held in Marrakech in 1997, The Hague in 2000, and Kyoto in 2003 perpetuated the dichotomy in approach between characterizing water as a right and as a need.

It is worth mentioning in this connection that the ICESCR, which provided the basis for the recognition of the human right to water, was adopted by the General Assembly of the United Nations in 1966, more than a decade before the Mar del Plata Water Conference. Yet, it would take more than 35 years from its adoption before a wider and more elaborate interpretation, recognizing a human right to water, would be rendered by the Committee on Economic, Social and Cultural Rights to the phrases "adequate standard of living" in Article 11, and "the highest attainable standards of mental and physical health" in Article 12 of the ICESCR. In fact, the Committee's analysis reached further back chronologically, basing its recognition of the human right to water partly on certain key provisions of the UDHR that was adopted in 1948, and reaffirming the central place of water in the rights to life and the primordial principle of human dignity enshrined in the UDHR. Recognition of the human right to water by the Committee on Economic, Social and Cultural Rights in its 2002 General Comment No. 15 has heightened the debate on the issue of the human right to water.

Although it is conceded that General Comments are not binding *per se,* because the Committee has no authority to establish *new* obligations under the ICESCR, it is argued that General Comments provide a critical mechanism for developing a normative and contextualized understanding of the provisions of the ICESCR. The Study goes on to examine the analytic devices employed by the Committee: derivation and inference of the right to water from the relevant Articles of the ICESCR, proof of the centrality and necessity of water to the realization of other rights under the ICESCR, and prior recognition of the right to water in a number of other international legal instruments. In this, the Study underscores the fact that in General Comment No.15, the Committee is not creating new obligations for the States Parties to the ICESCR, but rather extrapolating the nature of their existing obligations.

It is also worth noting that it took the Committee on Economic, Social and Cultural Rights about 13 years between the time it issued the first General Comment in 1989, and General Comment No. 15 recognizing a human right to water in 2002. During those years, the world community had given increased attention to water resources management due to the vast array of problems faced in this sector. A large number of conferences and forums have been held, and resolutions and declarations have been adopted by those forums. Similarly, the General Assembly of the United Nations adopted a number of resolutions on issues related to water resources. As will be discussed in more detail later, such resolutions include those on the Right to Development, the International Year of Freshwater, the Millennium Development Goals, as well as International Decade for Action, 'Water for Life' 2005–2015. It is noteworthy that only one of these resolutions specifically proclaims a human right to water. Additionally, the work of the International Law Commission on the United Nations Convention on the Law of the Non-Navigational Uses of International Watercourses was completed in 1994, and the Convention was adopted by the General Assembly in May 1997. The Convention itself has contributed to the debate by mandating that special regard be given to the requirement of "vital human needs."

Those developments must undoubtedly have influenced the thinking within the Committee, leading to the issuance of General Comment No. 15. Furthermore, those developments are likely to strengthen the momentum contributed to by the General Comment and the other resolutions and declarations, bolstering the legal basis upon which the Committee based its recognition of a human right to water. Another value-added of those developments in general, and the General Comment in particular, is that they reinforce the impetus for the international and civil society organizations to move forward their efforts to translate the voluminous soft law commitments into legally binding, domestic law instruments. Such efforts are showing slow but steady progress, translated in the adoption of legislation, and the taking of action, by some countries in the direction of recognizing a human right to water.

PART ONE
Genesis of the Debate on the Right to Water

Recognition by the world community of the seriousness of the problems facing the water resources sector, and the attempts to address them, including the issue of the right to water, started in earnest in the 1970s, and have continued ever since. In 1972 the United Nations Conference on the Human Environment, held in Stockholm, identified water as one of the natural resources that needed to be safeguarded. Principle 2 of the Stockholm Declaration on Human Environment states that "the natural resources of the earth including the air, water, land, flora and fauna and especially representative samples of natural ecosystems must be safeguarded for the benefit of the present and future generations through careful planning or management, as appropriate."[13]

Five years later in 1977, the United Nations held the Mar del Plata Water Conference in Argentina. The Conference, devoted exclusively to discussing the emerging water resources problems, issued the Mar del Plata Action Plan, which was designed to address those problems.[14] The Action Plan included a number of recommendations and resolutions, covering a broad spectrum of issues. The recommendations dealt with various issues including assessment of water resources; water use and efficiency; environment, health, and pollution control; policy, planning, and management; and regional and international cooperation. The resolutions addressed areas such as assessment of water resources, community water supply, agricultural water use, research and development, river commissions,

---

[13] For the full text of the Stockholm Declaration see Declaration of the United Nations Conference on the Human Environment, June 16, 1972, U.N. Doc. A/CONF.48/14/Rev.1, Sales No. E. 73.II.A.14 (1973); reprinted in 11 I.L.M. 1416 (1972). See also Harald Hohmann, Basic Documents of International Environmental Law, 21 (Graham and Trotman 1992).

[14] See Report of the United Nations Water Conference, Mar del Plata, March 14–25, 1977, U.N. Publication, Sales No. E.77.II.A.12 (1977). The United Nations General Assembly adopted on December 19, 1977, the Report of the United Nations Water Conference and approved the Mar del Plata Action Plan as well as the other agreements reached at the Conference. The General Assembly also urged the member states and all organizations of the United Nations system to take intensified and sustained action for the implementation of the agreements reached at the Conference. See U.N. Resolution 32/158, 107th Plenary Meeting, December 19, 1977.

international cooperation, and water policies in the occupied territories. One critical outcome of the Conference was the agreement, as part of the Action Plan, to proclaim the period 1981 to 1990 as the "International Drinking Water Supply and Sanitation Decade" during which governments would assume a commitment to bring about substantial improvements in the drinking water supply and sanitation sectors.[15]

The debate on the right to water can be traced to this Conference. Resolution II on "Community Water Supply" declared for the first time that "All peoples, whatever their stage of development and their social and economic conditions, have the right to have access to drinking water in quantities and of a quality equal to their basic needs."[16] The Resolution went on to restate the universal recognition that availability of water and, to a significant extent, the disposal of waste water, are essential both for life and the full development of man, as an individual and as an integral part of society. To meet this challenge, the Resolution called for full international cooperation, entailing the mobilization of physical, economic, and human resources, ". . . so that water is attainable and is justly and equitably distributed among the people within the respective countries."[17]

---

[15] The Report of the United Nations Water Conference urged that the Decade ". . . should be devoted to implementation of the national plans for drinking water supply and sanitation in accordance with the Plan of Action contained in Resolution II below. This implementation will require a concerted effort by countries and the international community to ensure a reliable drinking water supply and provide basic facilities to *all* urban and rural communities . . ." (emphasis added). *See id.*, at 14. The United Nations General Assembly did not refer in Resolution 32/158 (adopting the Report of the United Nations Water Conference, *see supra* n. 14) to the recommendation of the U.N. Water Conference designating the decade of 1981–1990 as the International Drinking Water Supply and Sanitation Decade. However, this matter was addressed by the General Assembly in a later resolution in 1980. Resolution 35/18, adopted by the General Assembly on November 10, 1980, at the 55th Plenary Meeting, after referring to the Mar del Plata Action Plan, proclaimed "the period 1981–1990 as the International Drinking Water Supply and Sanitation Decade, during which Member States will assume a commitment to bring about a substantial improvement in the standards and levels of services in drinking water supply and sanitation by the year 1990." The Resolution went on to call upon governments to develop the necessary policies, set targets, and mobilize the necessary resources for this purpose. It also called upon the United Nations system and other intergovernmental and non-governmental organizations concerned to continue and, if possible, to increase their technical and financial cooperation with developing countries in order to enable them to attain the targets they have set. The United Nations General Assembly followed up on the matter and issued Resolution 40/171 on December 17, 1985, at its 119th Plenary Meeting, as a middle-of-the-Decade reminder to the states that "significant progress towards meeting the objectives of the Decade by 1990 will require a much greater sense of urgency and priority on the part of Governments and the continued support of the international community."

[16] *See* Report of the United Nations Water Conference, *supra* n. 14, Resolution II (a), at 66.

[17] *See id.*, Resolution II (e), at 67.

The Resolution unquestionably represented a milestone, particularly considering the time at which it was issued, a quarter of a century before the United Nations Committee on Economic, Social and Cultural Rights declared safe drinking water a human right. Referring simply to a "right" rather than a "human right," the Resolution clearly addressed the issues related to the right of access to safe drinking water. As such, the Mar del Plata Water Conference can be considered the starting point for the debate on the right to water, and it has indeed provided the basis for the current discussion on the issue of the human right to water.

The world community's attempts to deal with water problems continued in a series of conferences that have been held since that time. In January 1992 the International Conference on Water and the Environment was held in Dublin, Ireland, and issued the Dublin Statement on Water and Sustainable Development.[18] Principle 4 of the Dublin Statement proclaims that "water has an economic value in all its competing uses and should be recognized as an economic good."[19] Yet the Statement clarified that within this principle "it is vital to recognize first the basic right of all human beings to have access to clean water and sanitation at an affordable price."[20] Read together, the Dublin Principles confirmed the right to water *at an affordable price*. Thus, the right to water does not necessarily mean that water should be provided free of charge. However, the Dublin Principles do not explain the concept of "affordability," nor do they suggest means through which its content and meaning could be determined.

The Dublin Conference was a preparatory meeting for the United Nations Conference on Environment and Development (UNCED) that was held in Rio de Janeiro, Brazil, in June 1992 (the Rio Summit). Agenda 21 of the Rio Summit, "Programme of Action for Sustainable Development," included a separate chapter (Chapter 18) on freshwater resources.[21] The overall objective laid down

---

[18] For the Dublin Statement on Water and Sustainable Development, *see* Journal of Water SRT, Aqua, Vol. 41, No. 3, at 129. The Dublin Statement consists of three main parts: The Guiding Principles, The Action Agenda, and The Enabling Environment, in addition to the introduction and the final part titled "Follow-Up."

[19] The other three principles state: (i) fresh water is a finite and vulnerable resource, essential to sustain life, development and the environment, (ii) water development and management should be based on a participatory approach, involving users, planners, and policy makers at all levels, and (iii) women play a central part in the provision, management, and safeguarding of water. *See id.*, at 129.

[20] *See id.*, 130.

[21] *See Earth Summit, Agenda 21, The United Nations Programme of Action from Rio*, U.N. ISBN 92: 92-1-100509-4; Sales No. E.93.1.11, 166 (United Nations Publication 1993). The

for freshwater resources is "to satisfy the freshwater needs of all countries for their sustainable development." On the issue of the needs and rights to water, Chapter 18 stated that ". . . water resources have to be protected, taking into account the functioning of aquatic ecosystems and the perenniality of the resources, in order to satisfy and reconcile needs for water in human activities. In developing and using water resources, priority has to be given to the satisfaction of basic needs and the safeguarding of the ecosystems."[22] Moreover, Chapter 18 endorsed the Resolution of the Mar del Plata Water Conference that all peoples have the right to have access to drinking water, and called this "the commonly agreed premise."[23]

The continued realization by the world community of the seriousness of the problems facing water resources resulted in the establishment in 1996 of the World Water Council (WWC)[24] and the Global Water Partnership (GWP).[25] The WWC is supposed to act as a think tank on water resources matters, while the GWP is established as a working partnership among all entities involved in water to support countries in integrated water resources management. Those two institutions led the work that resulted in the holding of the First World Water Forum in Marrakech, Morocco, in 1997,[26] the Second World Water Forum in The Hague, the Netherlands, in 2000,[27] and the third one in Kyoto,

---

title of Chapter 18 is "Protection of the Quality and Supply of Freshwater Resources: Application of integrated approaches to the development, management and use of water resources."

[22] *See id.*, paragraph 18.8, at 167. Being a conference on "Environment and Development," it is not surprising that the issue of "ecosystem" was equated with human "basic needs."

[23] *See id.*, paragraph 18.47, at 175. It is worth mentioning that, despite the special attention given to water at the Rio Conference (UNCED), the *Rio Declaration on Environment and Development,* U.N. Doc. A/CONF.151/26/Rev. 1 (1992); 31 I.L.M. 874 (1992), does not contain a specific reference to water.

[24] For more details on the World Water Council *see* <http://www.worldwatercouncil.org/>.

[25] For more details on the Global Water Partnership *see* <http://www.gwpforum.org/servlet/PSP>.

[26] For the proceedings of the First World Water Forum *see Water, the World's Common Heritage—Proceedings of the First World Water Forum, Marrakesh, Morocco,* (Mohamed Aït-Kadi, Aly Shady & Andras Szöllösi-Nagy, eds., Elsevier 1997). The different documentation on this Forum spells "Marrakech" sometimes as "Marrakesh." One of the outcomes of the Marrakech meeting was the establishment of the World Commission for Water in the 21st Century (WCW), which was entrusted with preparing a global vision for water, and presenting it at the Second World Water Forum. The WCW prepared and presented its vision in a report entitled "A Water Secure World." *See infra* n. 259.

[27] For The Hague Water Forum *see* <http://www.waterlink.net/gb/secWWF.htm>.

Japan, in 2003.[28] The Marrakech Declaration, which was issued at the end of the First World Water Forum on March 22, 1997, did not go as far as Mar del Plata, Dublin, or Rio with regard to the right to drinking water. It merely recommended "action to recognize the basic human needs to have access to clean water and sanitation."[29] A similar statement was included in the Ministerial Declaration of The Hague, which called for recognition "that access to safe and sufficient water and sanitation are basic human needs."[30] The Kyoto Ministerial Declaration missed the issue altogether, only stating that ". . . we will enhance poor people's access to safe drinking water and sanitation."[31]

The vacillation between declaring water a basic human need or a human right was further highlighted by the General Assembly of the United Nations. In 1999, the General Assembly issued a resolution on "The Right to Development."[32] The Resolution affirmed the right to development, as established in the Declaration on the Right to Development, as universal and inalienable, and reemphasized that its promotion, protection, and realization are an integral part of the promotion and protection of all human rights. The Resolution reaffirmed that, in the realization of the right to development, *inter alia*, "the rights to food and clean water are fundamental human rights and their promotion constitutes a moral imperative both for national Governments and for the international community."[33] This statement, no doubt, is the strongest and

---

[28] For the Kyoto Water Forum *see* <http://www.world.water-forum3.com>. *See also* François Guerquin, Tarek Ahmed, Mi Hua, Tetsuya Ikeda, Vedat Ozbilen & Marlies Schuttelaar, *World Water Actions, Making Water Flow for All* (Water Action Unit, World Water Council 2003).

[29] *See* Mohamed Aït-Kadi et al., *supra* n. 26, at 16.

[30] For the Ministerial Declaration of The Hague *see* <http://www.waterlink.net/gb/secwwf12.htm>.

[31] For the Kyoto Ministerial Declaration *see* <http://www.world.water-forum3.com/jp/mc/md_info.html>.

[32] *See* A/Res/54/175 of December 17, 1999 (83rd Plenary Meeting). This resolution should be distinguished from the Declaration on the Right to Development *see infra* n. 75. One reason as to why the General Assembly issued a resolution bearing, more or less, the same title can be found in Recital 16 of this Resolution, which expressed the concern that ". . . The Declaration on the Right to Development is insufficiently disseminated," and noted that the Declaration ". . . should be taken into account, as appropriate, in bilateral and multilateral cooperation programmes, national development strategies and policies and activities of international organizations."

[33] *See id.*, paragraph 12. In addition to food and clean water, the paragraph stated that the right to shelter is also a basic human right. Moreover, the paragraph stated that "Health is essential

most unambiguous in declaring a human right to water, and linking this right to the overall right to development.

The resolutions, declarations, and action plans discussed above are statements of policy that do not possess formal legal enforceability.[34] In this respect, they should be distinguished from the conventions and treaties that are subject to signature and ratification, and that, once in force, are legally binding on the states that have ratified them. Resolutions and declarations are not subject to signing and ratification, and as such do not create binding effects, though they may provide the impetus for later binding instruments and further the definition of policy and principle in a given area.

A treaty that addresses the issue of water as a human need is the United Nations Convention on the Law of the Non-Navigational Uses of International Watercourses, which was adopted by the United Nations General Assembly on May 21, 1997.[35] Paragraph 1 of Article 10 of the Convention on the "relationship between different kinds of uses," states that in the absence of agreement or custom to the contrary, no use of an international watercourse enjoys priority over other uses.[36] Paragraph 2 states that "In the event of a conflict between uses of an international watercourse, it shall be resolved with reference to Articles 5 to 7 of the Convention, with special regard being given to the requirement of vital human needs." Article 5 of the Convention deals with equitable and reasonable utilization and participation. Article 6 lays down the factors relevant to equitable and reasonable utilization, and Article 7 deals with the obligation not to cause significant harm.

Article 10 has a lengthy historical background dating back to the early discussion within the International Law Commission (ILC) before the final parameters

---

for sustainable development," and education is "an essential factor for the political, social, cultural and economic development of all people."

[34] For a detailed discussion of those resolutions and declarations, *see* Salman M. A. Salman, *From Marrakech Through The Hague to Kyoto—Has the Global Debate on Water Reached a Dead End? Part One,* 28 Water International, 491 (2003); and *Part Two,* 29 Water International, 11 (2004).

[35] The Convention was adopted by a vote of 103 for, and 3 against (Burundi, China, and Turkey) with 27 abstentions. Fifty-two countries did not participate in the voting. For the text of the Convention, *see* 36 I.L.M. 700 (1997). *See also International Watercourses, Enhancing Cooperation and Managing Conflict,* 173 (Salman M. A. Salman & Laurence Boisson de Chazournes, eds.,) World Bank Technical Paper No. 414, Annex 1, (1998).

[36] Navigation enjoyed priority over other uses during the nineteenth and the early years of the twentieth century, *see* Lucius Caflisch, *Regulation of the Uses of International Watercourses,* in Salman M. A. Salman and Laurence Boisson de Chazournes, eds., *supra* n. 35, at 6–7. *See also* Stephen McCaffrey, *The Law of International Watercourses—Non-Navigational Uses,* 311 (Cambridge University Press 2001), and Salman M. A. Salman & Kishor Uprety, *Conflict*

of the draft Convention were agreed upon.[37] Although one of the factors for determining equitable and reasonable utilization in Article 6 of the Convention relates to "the social and economic needs of the watercourse States concerned,"[38] there was concern within the ILC Drafting Committee about the absence of a priority principle concerning the list of those relevant factors. To address this matter, the Committee in 1991 suggested that, among the factors to be taken into account in solving a conflict between uses, special attention should be given to the supply of water needed to sustain human life, including drinking water or water required for the production of food.[39] This explanation was accepted by the Working Group, which added the following statement of understanding regarding article 10 (2):

> In determining "vital human needs", special attention is to be paid to providing sufficient water to sustain human life, including both drinking water and water required for production of food in order to prevent starvation.[40]

---

and Cooperation on South Asia's International Rivers—A Legal Perspective 8–11 (Kluwer Law International 2002).

[37] On December 8, 1970, the United Nations General Assembly adopted Resolution 2669 (XXV) asking the International Law Commission (ILC) to study the topic of international watercourses. The ILC started working on the draft Convention at its twenty-third session in 1971, and completed its work and adopted the articles of the draft Convention on June 24, 1994, and recommended the draft articles to the General Assembly on that date. The drafting of the Convention passed through a series of rapporteurs and reports at the ILC during the period 1971–1994. *See 1994 Yearbook of the International Law Commission*, Vol. II, Part Two, 88 (United Nations Publications 1997). For a detailed discussion of the issue, *see* Attila Tanzi & Maurizio Arcari, *The United Nations Convention on the Law of International Watercourses,* 38 (Kluwer Law International 2001).

[38] Article 6 (1) of the Convention states that utilization of an international watercourse in an equitable and reasonable manner within the meaning of Article 5 requires taking into account all relevant factors and circumstances, including:

(a) geographic, hydrographic, hydrological, climatic, ecological, and other factors of a natural character;

(b) social and economic needs of the watercourse states concerned;

(c) population dependent on the watercourse in the watercourse state;

(d) the effects of the use or uses of the watercourses in one watercourse state on other watercourse states;

(e) existing and potential uses of the watercourses;

(f) conservation, protection, development, and economy of the water resources of the watercourse and the cost of measures taken to that effect; and

(g) availability of alternatives, of comparable value, to a particular planned or existing use.

For the provisions of the Convention *see supra* n. 35.

[39] *See* Attila Tanzi & Maurizio Arcari, *supra* n. 37, at 139.

[40] *See* Report of the Sixth Committee convening as the Working Group of the Whole, April 11, 1997, U.N. Doc.A/51/869, at 5; reproduced in Stephen McCaffrey, *supra* n. 36, at 311, and Attila Tanzi & Maurizio Arcari, *supra* n. 37, at 139.

Thus, the U.N. Watercourses Convention does not directly address the issue of the human right to water. Rather, it confined its concerns to the issue of "vital human needs," the meaning and practical implications of which are still difficult to articulate.[41]

All of the conferences and forums that were held during the 1980s and 1990s issued declarations, resolutions, and detailed action plans aimed at addressing water problems. The most notable of these was the United Nations Millennium Declaration, issued on September 8, 2000. The Declaration was adopted unanimously by the General Assembly of the United Nations, and was signed by the 147 heads of states who attended the Millennium Summit. The Declaration addressed eight Millennium Development Goals to be achieved by the year 2015. Those goals include reducing by half the proportion of people without sustainable access to safe drinking water.[42] The United Nations Summit on Sustainable

---

[41] The U.N. Watercourses Convention has not yet entered into force. At the time of completing this Study (March 2004), 16 countries had signed the Convention, and only 12 countries had ratified or acceded to the Convention. For the current status of signing, ratification of, and accession to the Convention, *see* <http://untreaty.un.org/ENGLISH/bible/englishinternetbible/partI/chapterXXVII/treaty40.asp>. The Convention needs 35 instruments of ratification to enter into force; *see* Article 36 of the Convention.

[42] For the Millennium Declaration and the Millennium Development Goals *see* <http://www.developmentgoals.org/>. The eight millennium development goals are: (i) eradication of extreme poverty and hunger, (ii) achievement of universal primary education, (iii) promotion of gender equality and empowering women, (iv) reducing child mortality, (v) improving maternal health, (vi) combating HIV/AIDS, malaria, and other diseases, (vii) ensuring environmental sustainability, and (viii) developing global partnership for development. The goal of reducing by half the proportion of people without sustainable access to safe drinking water is actually part of the seventh goal of ensuring environmental sustainability. The other part of this goal relates to integrating the principles of sustainable development into country policies and programs and reversing the loss of environmental resources. It is worth noting that water is a central element to the first goal of eradicating extreme poverty and hunger, because most poor people live in dry areas, and because water is an essential element for growing food for eradicating hunger. It is also worth noting that water is quite relevant to the fourth goal (reducing child mortality), and the fifth goal (improving maternal health). Indeed, water-related diseases are a major problem, particularly in the developing world, and are thought to have "caused 3.4 million deaths in 1998, more than half of them children. Other estimates are even higher, particularly for diarrhoea." *See* William J. Cosgrove & Frank R. Rijsberman, *supra* n. 2 at 4. The World Health Organization (WHO) and the United Nations Children's Fund (UNICEF) state that diarrhea has killed more children in the last 10 years than all those lost to armed conflict since World War II, and that a child dies every 15 seconds from diarrhea, caused largely by poor sanitation and water supply. *See* WHO and UNICEF Joint Monitoring Program on Water Supply and Sanitation, Assessment 2000 Report. In Part IV of the Millennium Declaration, dealing with Protecting Our Common Environment, the parties resolved in paragraph 23 to "stop the unsustainable exploitation of water resources by developing water

Development that was held in Johannesburg in September 2002 added a similar goal with regard to basic sanitation.[43]

In addition to the Resolution on the Right to Development issued in 1999, and the Millennium Declaration issued in 2000, the General Assembly of the United Nations adopted two other resolutions on water resources. In December 2000, the General Assembly issued a resolution proclaiming the year 2003 as the "International Year of Freshwater."[44] The other resolution, "International Decade for Action, 'Water for Life' 2005–2015," was adopted in December 2003.[45] After referring to the Millennium Declaration and the Johannesburg Plan of Implementation, the Resolution proclaimed the period 2005 to 2015 as the International Decade for Action, Water for Life, and stated that the period would commence on World Water Day, March 22, 2005.[46] The Resolution further stated that the goals of the Decade should include "a greater focus on water related issues, at all levels, and on the implementation of water related programs and projects . . . in order to achieve internationally agreed water related goals . . ."[47]

The resolutions emanating from the various water conferences and forums vacillated between treating the issue of access to water as a basic need and as a right,[48] but no attempt was made to define either term, or to distinguish them

---

management strategies at the regional, national, and local levels, which promote both equitable access and adequate supplies."

[43] For the Johannesburg Summit *see* <http://www.johannesburgsummit.org>. It is unfortunate that the Millennium Development Goal with regard to water missed the issue of sanitation. The Johannesburg Summit has corrected this oversight by adding sanitation to this goal, thus underscoring the importance of integrating water and sanitation. It should also be recalled that the Mar del Plata Water Conference addressed both water and sanitation.

[44] Resolution 55/196 (87th Plenary Meeting, December 20, 2000).

[45] Resolution 58/217 (78th Plenary Meeting, December 23, 2003).

[46] The General Assembly of the United Nations decided on December 22, 1992 (A/Res/47/193), "to declare 22 March of each year World Day for Water, to be observed starting in 1993, in conformity with the recommendations of the United Nations Conference on Environment and Development contained in chapter 18 of Agenda 21." *See id.*, paragraph 1. The Resolution further invited the States "to devote the Day, as appropriate in the national context, to concrete activities such as the promotion of public awareness through the publication and diffusion of documentaries and the organization of conferences, round tables, seminars and expositions related to the conservation and development of water resources and the implementation of the recommendations of Agenda 21." *See id.*, paragraph 2.

[47] *See supra* n. 45, paragraph 2.

[48] Reference should also be made in this connection to two other international conferences. The first is the Water and Sustainable Development International Conference that was held in Paris, France, in March 1998. The Programme of Priority Actions underscored the fact that

from one another. The term "need" implies some sense of charity, and represents the recipients as passive beneficiaries, whereas "right" conveys a sense of legal entitlement, which should, in turn, result in a corresponding duty. Of particular note for this Study is the fact that those resolutions and declarations, except the United Nations General Assembly Resolution on the Right to Development discussed above, stop short of an explicit proclamation of a human right to water. The debate on the issue of the human right to water, and how to give effect to it, was heightened in November 2002, with the Committee on Economic, Social and Cultural Rights declaration that "The human right to water entitles everyone to sufficient, safe, acceptable, physically accessible and affordable water for personal and domestic uses"[49] as will be discussed in the third and fourth Parts of this Study.

"water resources are essential for satisfying human needs, health, food production, and the preservation of ecosystems. . . ." For the Programme of Priority Actions *see* <http://www.waternunc.com/gb/decfingb.htm>. The second is the Ministerial Session of the International Conference on Freshwater that was held in Bonn, Germany, in December 2000. The Ministerial Declaration of the Bonn meeting pronounced safe and sufficient drinking water and sanitation as basic human needs. For the text of the Bonn Ministerial Declaration *see* <http://www.water-2001.de/outcome/MinistersDeclaration/Ministerial_Declaration.pdf>. At the regional level, "The Abuja Ministerial Declaration on Water—A Key to Sustainable Development" was issued on April 30, 2002, by the African ministers responsible for water resources in their respective countries, at the end of their meeting in Abuja, Nigeria. The Abuja Declaration stated in paragraph 4 (a) that "An adequate supply of freshwater is the most important prerequisite for sustaining human life, for maintaining ecosystems that support all life, and for achieving sustainable development." For the Abuja Ministerial Declaration, *see* <http://www.thewaterpage.com/Documents/amcow_declaration.pdf>. *See also* Salman M. A. Salman, *The Abuja Ministerial Declaration—A Milestone or Just Another Statement?* 27 Water International 442 (2002).

[49] *See* paragraph 2 of General Comment No. 15, *infra* n. 198.

PART TWO
Evolution of the International Legal Regime for Human Rights

Early Developments

Although a number of important precursors exist,[50] the modern history of what Thomas Buergenthal calls "contemporary international human rights law"[51] or what Henkin terms "the new law of human rights"[52] is properly traced to the United Nations Charter.[53] The Charter was passed by the General Assembly of

---

[50] Among these are the Magna Carta (1215), the English Bill of Rights (1689), the French Declaration on the Rights of Man and Citizen (1789) and the United States Constitution and Bill of Rights (1791). For an insightful account of the modern history of international human rights from pre-World War I to World War II, *see* Frank Newman, Joan Fitzpatrick & David Weissbrodt, *International Human Rights: Law, Policy and Process,* 2–8 (3d ed., Anderson Publishing 2001). For a summary of antecedents of modern human rights law, *see* Thomas Buergenthal, *International Human Rights in a Nutshell*, 1–20 (2d ed. West Pub. Co. 1995).

[51] Thomas Buergenthal, *The Normative and Institutional Evolution of International Human Rights*, 19 Hum. Rts. Q. 703 (1997). *See also* Antonio Cassese, *Human Rights in a Changing World*, 9–48 (Temple University Press 1990), and A. H. Robertson & J. G. Merrils, *Human Rights in the World: An Introduction to the Study of the International Protection of Human Rights*, Chs. 1 & 2, 1–54 (4th ed., Manchester University Press 1997).

[52] Louis Henkin, *supra* n. 3, at 6–11.

[53] The instruments focused on in this book are not only "contemporary," but they are also largely "Western" in terms of the values they emphasize and the processes they rely upon. In this connection, it should be noted that a large body of influential non-Western conceptions of human rights exist. For a discussion of non-Western conceptions of human rights, *see The East Asian Challenge for Human Rights* (Joanne R. Bauer & David A. Bell, eds., Cambridge University Press 1999); *Asian Perspectives on Human Rights* (Claude E. Welch & Virginia A. Leary, eds., Westview Press 1990). For a critique from an African perspective *see* Makua Mutua, *Human Rights: A Political and Cultural Critique* (University of Pennsylvania Press 2002); Yougindra Khushalani, *Human Rights in Asia and Africa*, 4 HRLJ 404, 414 (1983); Lakshman Marasinghe, *Traditional conceptions of human rights in Africa,* in *Human Rights and Development in Africa,* 32 (Claude Welch Jr. & Ronald Meltzer, eds., State University of New York Press 1984). *See also* Jack Donnelly, *Universal Human Rights in Theory and Practice* (Cornell University Press 1989), particularly Chapter 5, at 71–86, "Non-Western Conceptions of Human Rights" where the author discussed human rights in Islam, in traditional Africa, and China, as well as other systems. *See also* Chapter 6 on Cultural Relativism at 89–103. For a critique of the "noninclusive" nature of international human rights law, *see* Amitai Etzioni, *The New Golden Rule: Community and Morality in a Democratic Society*, 235–236 (Basic Books 1996).

the United Nations, and signed on June 26, 1945.[54] The preamble of the Charter proclaims the signatories' determination to "reaffirm faith in fundamental human rights, in the dignity and worth of the human person, in the equal rights of men and women and of nations large and small . . ."

Article 1 of the Charter sets forth the purposes of the United Nations, which include, *inter alia,* ". . . promoting and encouraging respect for human rights and for fundamental freedoms for all without distinction as to race, sex, language, or religion . . ." The Charter also introduces an important new principle in the notion that the relations between states and their own citizens were now a matter of international concern, and no longer the exclusive purview of sovereign states.[55] That being said, it is critical to note that the U.N. Charter retains a balance between the principles of sovereignty and non-interference and that of respect for human rights.[56] Those principles have continued to develop, and the relationship between them has likewise continued to evolve.

Building on their pledge to protect human rights, the members of the United Nations established the Commission on Human Rights in 1946, under the Eco-

---

[54] For the United Nations Charter *see* UKTS 1946 No. 67. *See also* <http://www.un.org/aboutun/charter/index.html>. It is worth noting that the League of Nations established the minorities system that Bertrand Ramcharan referred to as "the first building blocks for an international legal regime for the protection of human rights." *See* Bertrand Ramcharan, *The United Nations High Commissioner for Human Rights—The Challenges of International Protection*, 1 (Martinus Nijhoff Publishers 2002).

[55] The notion that the relations between states and their own nationals were now a matter of international concern did not imply the compromise of the concept of sovereignty, nor did it dispense with the need for state consent to the new human rights legal regime. *See* Louis Henkin, *International Law: Politics, Values and Functions*, in *216 Collected Courses of The Hague Academy of International Law*, Vol. IV, 215 (1989).

[56] Article 2(1): "The Organization is based on the principle of the sovereign equality of all its Members."

Article 2(7): "Nothing contained in the present Charter shall authorize the United Nations to intervene in matters which are essentially within the domestic jurisdiction of any state or shall require the Members to submit such matters to settlement under the present Charter; but this principle shall not prejudice the application of enforcement measures under Chapter VII." It is worth noting that prior to the U.N. Charter, Article 15(8) of the Covenant of the League of Nations prohibited the League from interfering in any member country's "domestic jurisdiction."

Article 1 enumerates the purposes of the United Nations, including "To develop friendly relations among nations based on respect for the principle of equal rights and self-determination of peoples, and to take other appropriate measures to strengthen universal peace; . . . To achieve international co-operation in solving international problems of an economic, social, cultural, or humanitarian character, and in promoting and encouraging respect for human rights and for fundamental freedoms for all without distinction as to race, sex, language, or religion."

nomic and Social Council (ECOSOC).[57] The initial task with which the Commission was entrusted was the drafting of an instrument articulating the nature and content of the human rights and freedoms that the United Nations had affirmed.[58] After two years of work, the Commission completed drafting the UDHR, which was adopted by the General Assembly of the United Nations on December 10, 1948.[59] The UDHR introduced a number of revolutionary concepts, not least of which was the notion of recognition of the inherent dignity and

---

Furthermore, Article 55 provides:

"With a view to the creation of conditions of stability and well-being which are necessary for peaceful and friendly relations among nations based on respect for the principle of equal rights and self-determination of peoples, the United Nations shall promote:

a. higher standards of living, full employment, and conditions of economic and social progress and development;

b. solutions of international economic, social, health, and related problems; and international cultural and educational cooperation; and

c. universal respect for, and observance of, human rights and fundamental freedoms for all without distinction as to race, sex, language, or religion."

[57] The Commission was established by ECOSOC Resolution 5 (1) of February 16, 1946. It is the only commission for which provision is made in the United Nations Charter. Article 68 of the Charter states that "The Economic and Social Council shall set up commissions in economic and social fields and for the promotion of human rights, and such other commissions as may be required for the performance of its functions." To support the work of the Commission, a Division of Human Rights was established as part of the United Nations Secretariat. This was later renamed as the Centre for Human Rights, and in 1997 was consolidated into the Office of the United Nations High Commissioner for Human Rights (OHCHR), (*see infra* n. 100). The Commission on Human Rights meets annually and, if required, convenes special sessions. The Commission also reports directly to ECOSOC. Shortly after its establishment, the Commission established a Sub-Commission on Prevention of Discrimination and Protection of Minorities to assist the Commission in its work. For more details on the work of the Commission on Human Rights *see* <http://www.unhchr.ch/html/menu2/2/chr.htm>.

[58] The Commission benefited from the indomitable leadership of Mrs. Eleanor Roosevelt who was elected Chairperson of the Commission by its Delegates; *see generally*, Mary Ann Glendon, *A World Made New: Eleanor Roosevelt and the Universal Declaration of Human Rights* (Random House 2001).

[59] The UDHR was adopted and proclaimed by General Assembly Resolution 217 A (III) of December 10, 1948. For the text of the UDHR *see* General Assembly Resolution GA res. 217 A (III), U.N. Doc. A/810 at 71 (1948). *See also* appendix I to this Study. The literature devoted to the Universal Declaration is voluminous. Noteworthy examples include Johannes Morsink, *The Universal Declaration of Human Rights: Origins, Drafting, and Intent (Pennsylvania Studies in Human Rights)* (University of Pennsylvania Press 1999); A. Cassese, *supra* n. 51, at 24–47. Of the 58 members of the General Assembly in 1948, 48 members voted in favor of the UDHR (two absentees), and the remaining eight members abstained; *see* Johannes Morsink, *id.*, at 11–12. *See also* the Office of the United Nations High Commissioner for Human Rights, *The Universal Declaration of Human Rights: A Magna Carta for all humanity*, (United Nations Department of Public Information, DPI/1937/A 1997) at <http://www.unhchr.ch/udhr/miscinfo/carta.htm>.

the equal and inalienable rights of all persons, as well as the idea that human rights are both universal and international.[60] Article 1 proclaims that "All human beings are born free and equal in dignity and rights" and is followed by 29 articles covering core civil and political rights[61] and economic, social, and cultural rights.[62] It is also worth noting that alongside the extensive catalogue of rights embodied in the UDHR, the instrument also made provision for *duties*. Article 29 (1) provides "Everyone has duties to the community in which alone the free and full development of his personality is possible."[63]

While only a declaration, and not intended to bind States at the time it was proclaimed, some commentators now contend that certain provisions of the UDHR are part of customary international law and binding to that extent.[64] The focus of inquiry in this connection has shifted to *which* of its provisions have the status of customary international law, rather than *whether* they do. As Henkin has aptly observed, "Few claim that any state that violates any provision of the Declaration has violated international law. Almost all would agree that some violations of the

---

[60] *See* the Preamble to the UDHR. As Robertson and Merrils state, "The protection of human rights through international action is a revolutionary idea and traditional international law had no place for it at all." *See supra* n. 51, at 1.

[61] Included in the civil and political rights under the UDHR are the principle of equality before the law and the entitlement without any discrimination to equal protection of the law (Article 7), the right to fair and public hearing (Article 10), and the presumption of innocence (Article 11). The UDHR also proclaims the right not to be subjected to arbitrary interference with one's privacy, family, home, or correspondence, nor to attacks on one's honor or reputation (Article 12); the right to freedom of opinion and expression (Article 19); and the right of freedom of peaceful assembly and association (Article 20).

[62] Among the core economic, social, and cultural rights proclaimed under the UDHR are the right to work, to free choice of employment, to just and favorable conditions of work, and to protection against unemployment (Article 23); the right to a standard of living adequate for the health and well-being of oneself and one's family, (Article 25); and the right to education (Article 26). The UDHR also includes cultural rights such as the right to freely participate in the cultural life of the community, to enjoy the arts, and to share in scientific advancement and its benefits (Article 27).

[63] *See* Johannes Morsink, *The Philosophy of the Universal Declaration*, 6 Hum. Rts. Q. 309, 310–320 (1989) for a discussion of the history of the inclusion of Article 29 and the significance of the word "alone" specified there, as countering any excessive individualism in the UDHR and reinforcing the place of community in the human rights discourse, and underscoring the importance of the relationship between the individual and the society in which the individual lives.

[64] *See* Hurst Hannum, *The Status of the Universal Declaration of Human Rights in National and International Law*, 25 Ga. J. Int'l & Comp. L. 287, 317–352 (1995–1996). On human rights law and custom more generally, *see* Bruno Simma & Philip Alston, *The Sources of Human Rights Law: Custom, Jus Cogens and General Principles*, 12 Australian Yb. Int'l. L. 82 (1992).

Declaration are violations of international law."[65] In a more general sense, the UDHR has become a highly visible and widely recognized articulation of moral and political standards, and a measure by which respect for, and compliance with, international human rights principles can be judged.[66]

Once the UDHR was adopted, the Commission began drafting the treaties implementing, in substantive, enforceable terms, the more general commitments of the UDHR.[67] For political and ideological reasons, and because of procedural considerations pertaining to the enforcement and realization of the rights, as will be discussed later, it was decided that two separate covenants should be drawn up, each devoted to a different "aspect" of human rights. In 1954 the two Covenants were presented to the United Nations General Assembly, but 12 years would elapse before they would be adopted by the General Assembly. The International Covenant on Civil and Political Rights (ICCPR)[68] enumerates "negative," liberty-oriented rights that a state is bound to forbear interfering with, such as freedom of expression, freedom of conscience, and freedom of association.[69]

---

[65] Louis Henkin, *The Age of Rights,* 19 (Columbia University Press 1990).

[66] It should be noted that the Vienna Declaration emphasized that "the Universal Declaration of Human Rights, which constitutes a common standard of achievement for all peoples and all nations, is the source of inspiration and has been the basis for the United Nations in making advances in standard setting as contained in the existing human rights instruments . . ." *See* Preamble to the Vienna Declaration and Programme of Action (UNGA) (A/CONF.157/23), issued on July 12, 1993, by the United Nations World Conference on Human Rights, Vienna, Austria, June 14–25, 1993.

[67] It is worth mentioning, in this connection, that the first treaty for modern human rights is the Convention on the Prevention and Punishment of the Crime of Genocide (the Genocide Convention), 78 U.N.T.S. 277. The Convention was adopted by General Assembly Resolution 260 (III) A, on December 9, 1948, one day before the adoption of the Universal Declaration of Human Rights, and entered into force on January 12, 1951. Article II of the Convention defines genocide as "any of the following acts committed with intent to destroy, in whole or in part, a national, ethnical, racial or religious group, as such: (a) killing members of the group; (b) causing serious bodily or mental harm to members of the group; (c) deliberately inflicting on the group conditions of life calculated to bring about its physical destruction in whole or in part; (d) imposing measures intended to prevent births within the group; and (e) forcibly transferring children of the group to another group."

[68] For the ICCPR, *see* 6 I.L.M 368, (1967); *see also* 999 U.N.T.S 171, and appendix III to this Study. The ICCPR was adopted through United Nations General Assembly Resolution 2200A (XXI) of December 16, 1966, and entered into force March 23, 1976. Currently there are 159 signatories to the ICCPR, of which 151 countries have ratified the instrument. *See* <http://untreaty.un.org/ENGLISH/bible/englishinternetbible/partI/chapterIV/treaty6.asp>.

[69] The ICCPR prescribes a number of civil and political rights, including the right to life; the right against torture, cruel, inhuman, or degrading treatment; the right to liberty and security of person, and the right to be treated with humanity and respect when one is deprived of such a right; the right to recognition as a person before the law; the right to privacy; the right to

The International Covenant on Economic, Social and Cultural Rights (ICESCR)[70] addresses those aspects of the UDHR that pertain to people's basic rights,[71] such as food, shelter, and health care.[72]

Another distinction with regard to the two instruments is that of the "generations" of rights addressed. The ICESCR protects "second generation rights," while the ICCPR protects "first generation rights."[73] These terms evolved as a result of the relational position of economic, social, and cultural rights to civil and political rights.[74] Over time, however, these bifurcated concepts were challenged, and their

---

freedom of thought, conscience, and religion; the right to freedom of expression; the right to peaceful assembly and freedom of association; the right of the child; and the right against discrimination and to the equal protection of the law.

[70] For the ICESCR, *see* 6 I.L.M 360, (1967); *see also* 993 U.N.T.S 3, and appendix II to this Study. The ICESCR was adopted through United Nations General Assembly Resolution 2200A (XXI) of December 16, 1966, and entered into force January 3, 1976. Currently there are 155 signatories to the ICESCR, of which 148 countries have ratified the instrument. *See* <http://untreaty.un.org/ENGLISH/bible/englishinternetbible/partI/chapterIV/treaty5.asp>. It is noteworthy that the two instruments are termed "Covenants" and not "conventions" or "treaties." The reason is perhaps because the two Covenants deal largely with formal promises by states toward their citizens, and not with relationships between or among states. Black's Law Dictionary defines the term "Covenant" to mean "A formal agreement or promise, usu. in a contract." (*Black's Law Dictionary*, 7th ed., 1999, at 369).

[71] Although the ICESCR is based largely on the UDHR, Cranston noted that the ICESCR ". . . re-states in more cautious language most of the economic and social rights named in the Universal Declaration, and qualifies them in various ways, and . . . transfers certain rights from the individual person to what are referred to as 'peoples'." For further discussion of the differences between the UDHR and the ICESCR, *see* Maurice Cranston, *supra* n. 6, at 73. It is understandable that the States Parties would want to use more "temperate" language in the ICESCR than in the UDHR, with the former being a treaty, subject to signature and ratification, which commits parties to substantive legal undertakings.

[72] The ICESCR prescribes a number of rights, including the right to work that is freely chosen; the right of everyone to form trade unions; the right to social security, including social insurance; the right to adequate standard of living, including adequate food, clothing, and housing, and to the continuous improvement of living conditions; the right to be free from hunger; the right to the enjoyment of the highest attainable standard of physical and mental health; the right to education; the right to take part in cultural life, to enjoy the benefits of scientific progress and its applications, and to benefit from the protection of the moral and material interests resulting from any scientific, literary, or artistic production of which he is the author.

[73] For a full discussion of those sets of rights *see* Philip Alston, *Economic and Social Rights*, in *Human Rights: An Agenda for the Next Century*, 137–166 (Louis Henkin & John Lawrence Hargrove, eds., The American Society of International Law 1994); Philip Alston & Gerard Quinn, *The Nature and Scope of States Parties' Obligations under the International Covenant on Economic, Social and Cultural Rights*, 9 Hum. Rts. Q. 156–229 (1987); Matthew Craven, *The International Covenant on Economic, Social and Cultural Rights: A Perspective on its Development* (Clarendon Press 1995); *Guide to Interpretation of the International Covenant on Economic, Social and Cultural Rights*, Vols. I & II (Louis B. Sohn, ed., Transnational Publishers 1994).

[74] Other generations of rights have been identified beyond first and second generation rights. For discussion of those issues *see* Louis Henkin, *Other 'Generations' of Rights* in *International Law: Politics and Values*, 196–202 (Martinus Nijhoff Publishers 1995). As men-

traditional formulation critiqued as incapable of addressing key global issues. This led to the identification of "third generation rights" or "solidarity rights," the realization of which relies on the action of all actors, public and private alike. Examples of third generation rights include the right to a clean environment, the rights of communities, the right of self-determination, and the right to development.[75] Closely associated with the evolution of the right to development is the emergence of the concept of the rights-based approach to development, which, in the words of the Office of the High Commissioner for Human Rights, is

> a conceptual framework for the process of human development that is normatively based on international human rights standards and operationally directed to promoting and protecting human rights. Essentially, a rights-based approach integrates the norms, standards and principles of the international human rights system into the plans, policies and processes of development. The norms and standards are those contained in the wealth of international treaties and declarations. The principles include equality and equity, accountability, empowerment and participation. A rights-based approach to development includes the following elements: express linkage to rights, accountability, empowerment, participation, non-discrimination and attention to vulnerable groups.[76]

---

tioned above, these "third generation rights" include more collective, less individualistic rights such as the right to development, and, of particular relevance to this discussion, the right to a healthy environment.

[75] *See* Arjun Sengupta, *The Right to Development as a Human Right* (Working Paper Series, François-Xavier Center for Health and Human Rights, Harvard University 1999) at <http://www.hsph.harvard.edu/fxbcenter/FXBC_WP7—Sengupta.pdf>. There are two General Assembly resolutions proclaiming the right to development. The first resolution, Declaration on the Right to Development was adopted by General Assembly Resolution A/Res/41/128 of December 4, 1986. The second is General Assembly Resolution A/Res/54/175 of December 17, 1999 (*see supra* n. 32*).* In addition, General Assembly Resolution A/Res/48/141 of December 20, 1993, established the post of United Nations High Commissioner for Human Rights. This Resolution makes provision for the role of the High Commissioner in the realization of the right to development, *see especially* Sections 4 (c) and 7. In 1998, the Economic and Social Council, by its decision E/1998/269, endorsed the recommendation contained in Commission on Human Rights resolution 1998/72 of April 22, 1998, to establish a dual mechanism to explore in greater depth ways of implementing the right to development: an open-ended Working Group on the Right to Development and an independent expert on the right to development. The right to development was also noted in connection with UNGA Res. 41/117 (97th Plenary Meeting, December 4, 1986): Indivisibility and interdependence of economic, social, cultural, civil, and political rights, which recognized "that the realization of the right to development could help to promote the enjoyment of economic, social and cultural rights."

[76] *See* <http://www.unhchr.ch/development/approaches-04.html>. It is worth noting in this connection that the notion of the rights-based approach to development has received wide support and elaboration by the World Commission on Dams (WCD), which was established

Economic, social, and cultural rights are typically conceived as requiring positive action on the part of the state in the form of national policies and programs, while civil and political rights are viewed as directly endowed upon individuals, and secured primarily through governments refraining from interfering with them.[77] As Alston and Quinn observe:

> Economic, social and cultural rights require active intervention on the part of governments and cannot be realized without such intervention on the part of governments. Closely linked to this is a distinction between resource-intensive and cost-free rights. Thus, it is said that civil and political rights can be realized without significant costs being incurred, whereas the enjoyment of economic, social and cultural rights requires a major commitment of resources.[78]

Notwithstanding this, the distinction between the two kinds of rights should not, however, be overstated, because each category entails both positive as well as negative duties.[79] For example, the effective realization of a right to free speech may

---

as an *ad hoc* commission in 1997 to review the global experience with large dams. The WCD was critical of the traditional "balance sheet" approach of assessing costs and benefits of dam projects because it saw it as an inadequate tool for effective development planning and decisionmaking. Instead, the WCD recommended that an approach based on "recognition of rights" and "assessment of risks" be developed as a tool for guidance of future planning and decisionmaking, stressing that this approach would provide a more effective framework for integrating the economic, social, and environmental dimensions for options assessment and planning. The WCD identified five values to be addressed through this approach, namely, equity, efficiency, participatory decisionmaking, sustainability, and accountability. The WCD noted that "These values form the foundation of a rights-based approach to equitable decision-making about water and energy resources management." *See* World Commission on Dams, *Dams and Development—A New Framework for Decision-making (the Report of the World Commission on Dams)*, 206 (Earthscan Publications Ltd. 2000). The WCD stated that the United Nations Declaration on Human Rights, the Right to Development, and the Rio Declaration on Environment and Development "together make up an internationally accepted framework of norms empowering a concept of development that is economically viable, socially acceptable, and environmentally sustainable." *See id.,* at 202. For an overall analysis of the different aspects of the WCD Report *see Reactions to the Report of the World Commission on Dams*, 16 Am. U. Int'l L. Rev. 1411–1694 (2001).

[77] Asbjørn Eide & Allan Rosas, *Economic, Social and Cultural Rights: A Universal Challenge* in *Economic, Social and Cultural Rights, A Textbook*, 4–5 (Asbjørn Eide, Catarina Krause & Allan Rosas, eds., 2d ed., Martinus Nijhoff Publishers 2001).

[78] Philip Alston & Gerard Quinn, *supra* n. 73, at 159.

[79] McCaffrey doubts whether the immediate obligations to implement the rights under the ICCPR are absolute, "if only because implementation of some of the provisions of the Covenant may be economically impossible for poorer less developed countries." *See* Stephen McCaffrey, *A Human Right to Water: Domestic and International Implications*, 5 Geo. Intl. Envtl. L. Rev. 13 (1992). He agreed with Pierre-Marie Dupuy that the immediate requirement "is probably an obligation to exercise due diligence." *See* Pierre-Marie Dupuy, *Due Diligence*

require that the state actively promote the "public space" and channels of communication within which the right can be exercised freely and without interference from others. Conversely, the right to education may demand that the state refrain from interfering in the parents' right to inculcate values in their child. In this way, obligations of action and forbearance inhere in both sets of rights, and may pertain to private actors as well as the state. As Alston and Quinn opine:

> The main difference between the rights recognized in the two Covenants consists of the fact that the economic and social rights require relatively greater state action for their realization than do civil and political rights. This difference separates the two sets of rights more in terms of degree than in kind and the relative question to pose is not *whether* any particular kind requires positive action but rather the extent to which it can subsist as a meaningful right without such active state support. Given that the chief difference is one of degree, it can be said in general terms that economic and social rights are, on average, somewhat more dependant for their full realization on positive state action than are civil and political rights.[80]

Similarly, the nature of the obligations themselves is conceived as different. In contrast to those pertaining to the ICCPR, the obligations under the ICESCR are progressive in nature, as will be discussed in the next Part of this Study. Each State Party undertakes only to take steps to the maximum of its available resources with a view to progressively achieving the full realization of the rights recognized by all means appropriate.

Despite the issuance of two separate Covenants, with two discernible sets of rights, it is abundantly clear that the different categories of human rights are interrelated, interdependent, and indivisible, as stated, *inter alia,* in a number of General Assembly Resolutions,[81] as well as in the Vienna Declaration.[82] Thus, unless the basic social and economic standards necessary for subsistence are

---

in the International Law of Liability, in *Legal Aspects of Transfrontier Pollution*, 369 (Organisation for Economic Cooperation and Development 1977).

[80] Philip Alston & Gerard Quinn, *supra* n. 73, at 183–4.

[81] The General Assembly of the United Nations adopted a number of resolutions on, or addressing, the issue of indivisibility and interdependence of economic, social, cultural, civil, and political rights. Those resolutions include (i) Resolution 32/130: (105th Plenary Meeting, December 16, 1977), (ii) Resolution 40/114: (116th Plenary Meeting, December 13, 1985); (iii) Resolution 41/117: (97th Plenary Meeting, December 4, 1986) *see supra* n. 75; and (iv) Resolution A/Res/42/102: (93rd Plenary Meeting, December 7, 1987).

[82] For the Vienna Declaration and Programme of Action, *supra* n. 66.

maintained, the freedom protected by civil and political rights cannot be attained.[83] As noted by the General Assembly of the United Nations in its 1987 Resolution on the indivisibility and interdependence of economic, social, cultural, civil, and political rights:

> Recalling that in the Preambles to the International Covenants on Human Rights, it is recognized that the ideal of free human beings enjoying freedom from fear and want can only be achieved if conditions are created whereby persons may enjoy their economic, social and cultural rights, as well as their civil and political rights.[84]

Accordingly, each "category" of rights remains indispensable to the other, and no hierarchical categorization should be made between them.[85] The General Assembly gave this principle resounding endorsement in its Resolution on the indivisibility and interdependence of economic, social, cultural, civil, and political rights in 1987.[86] "Reaffirming the provisions of its resolution 32/130 of December 16, 1977 that all human rights and fundamental freedoms are indivisible and interdependent and that the protection and promotion of one category of rights can never exempt or excuse states from the promotion and protection of the other rights . . ." the Resolution went on to state that it was "Concerned that equal attention and urgent consideration should be given to the implementation, promotion and protection of economic, social, cultural, civil and political rights."[87]

---

[83] It has, however, been argued that the human right to life under the ICCPR is a civil right *only* and does not guarantee anyone against death from famine or cold or lack of medical attention. *See* Yoram Dinstein, *The Right to Life, Physical Integrity, and Liberty* in *The International Bill of Rights: The Covenant on Civil and Political Rights*, 114 (Louis Henkin, ed., Columbia University Press 1981). However, Hilal Elver argues that "The recent trend among human rights scholars is to expand the right of life under Article 6 (of the ICCPR) as much as possible. Under the right to life, in its modern and proper sense, not only is protection against any arbitrary deprivation of life upheld, but states are also under the duty to pursue policies that are designed to ensure access to the means of survival of every individual and for all peoples." *See* Hilal Elver, *Peaceful Uses of International Rivers—The Euphrates and Tigris Rivers Dispute*, 269 (Transnational Publishers, Inc. 2002).

[84] Preamble to UNGA Resolution on the Indivisibility and interdependence of economic, social, cultural, civil and political rights A/Res/42/102, *supra* n. 81. *See also* Henry J. Steiner & Philip Alston, *supra* n. 10, at 268–275.

[85] *See* Theo van Boven, *Distinguishing Criteria of Human Rights* in *The International Dimension of Human Rights* Vol. 1, 43 (Karel Vasak & Philip Alston, eds., Greenwood Press 1982).

[86] *See* Preamble to UNGA Resolution A/Res/42/102 on the Indivisibility and interdependence of economic, social, cultural, civil and political rights, *supra* n. 81. *See also* Henry J. Steiner & Philip Alston, *supra* n. 10, at 268–275.

[87] Resolution 32/130 dealt with "Alternative approaches and ways and means within the United Nations system for improving the effective enjoyment of human rights and funda-

Similarly, Paragraph 5 of the Vienna Declaration affirms that "All human rights are universal, indivisible and interdependent and interrelated. The international community must treat human rights globally in a fair and equal manner, on the same footing, and with the same emphasis . . ."[88] In this connection, Nobel laureate Amartya Sen has posed the following question: "What should come first—removing poverty and misery, or guaranteeing political liberty and civil rights, for which poor people have little use anyway? Is this a sensible way of approaching the problems of economic needs and political freedoms—in terms of a basic dichotomy that appears to undermine the relevance of political freedoms because the economic needs are so urgent?" In addressing those issues he observed:

> I would argue, no, this is altogether the wrong way to see the force of economic needs, or to understand the salience of political freedoms. The real issues that have to be addressed lie elsewhere, and they involve taking note of extensive interconnections between political freedoms and the understanding and fulfillment of economic needs. The connections are not only instrumental (political freedoms can have a major role in providing incentives and information in the solution of acute economic need), but also constructive. Our conceptualization of economic needs depends crucially on open public debates and discussions, the guaranteeing of which requires insistence on basic political liberty and civil rights.[89]

---

mental freedoms" adopted on the Reports of the Third Committee (105th Plenary Meeting, December 16, 1977), *supra* n. 81. Recital 1(a) states "All human rights and fundamental freedoms are indivisible and interdependent; equal attention and urgent consideration should be given to the implementation, promotion and protection of both civil and political, and economic, social and cultural rights."

[88] *See* Vienna Declaration and Programme of Action *supra* n. 66. Similarly, paragraph 8 of the Vienna Declaration states that "Democracy, development and respect for human rights and fundamental freedoms are interdependent and mutually reinforcing . . ." The notion of human rights being indivisible and interdependent was also proclaimed by the United Nations General Assembly seven years earlier in 1986 in the Declaration on the Right to Development (General Assembly Resolution 41/128 of December 4, 1986). Article 6 (2) of the Declaration states that "All human rights and fundamental freedoms are indivisible and interdependent; equal attention and urgent consideration should be given to the implementation, promotion and protection of civil, political, economic, social and cultural rights." For the Declaration on the Right to Development, *see* Edward Lawson, *Encyclopedia of Human Rights*, 361 (2d ed., Taylor and Francis 1996), *see also* <http://www.unhchr.ch/html/menu3/b/74.htm>.

[89] *See* Amartya Sen, *Development as Freedom*, 147–148 (Alfred A. Knopf, Inc. 1999). *See also* Amartya Sen, *Freedoms and Needs* in *The New Republic* 31, 32 (January 10–17, 1994). It is worth noting that what started as one group of human rights enunciated in the UDHR, and was later split into two categories of human rights, has ended up being interpreted and viewed again as indivisible and closely interrelated categories of human rights.

This is another, more recent authoritative statement on the interrelationship and interdependence of human rights, with which we are in full agreement. One objective of this Study is to highlight the necessity of the various rights to one another, and explain the profound and multitiered connections between them,[90] in the context of the human right to water.

Our submission on the interdependence and indivisibility of rights is a very simple one, and may be a truism; it is that neither set of rights has a full meaning without the other, and that attempting to find normative priority between them is a fruitless endeavor. This concurs with the message of President Roosevelt's famous "Four Freedoms" speech in which he proclaimed, in forceful and eloquent terms, the need for freedom of speech and expression, freedom to worship, freedom from want, and freedom from fear.[91]

Thus, the world community refined the general undertakings and aspirations of the provisions of the United Nations Charter on human rights into a specific international legal instrument, the UDHR, and about 30 years later, into two legally binding instruments, the ICESCR and the ICCPR. The prevailing understanding of human rights has evolved substantially since these instruments came into force, and with new global challenges and the emergence of new global actors such as international financial institutions, multinational corporations, and a better mobilized civil society, human rights law has had to evolve to meet these new challenges.

The International Covenants on Human Rights

One consequence of the distinction between the two sets of rights in the two international Covenants on human rights described above (the ICESCR and the ICCPR), is that the realization of the rights under the ICESCR is envisaged to be "achieved progressively."[92] This is because the rights provided for in the ICESCR

---

[90] On the normative interconnection of the two generations of rights, *see* Craig Scott, *The Interdependence and Permeability of Human Rights Norms: Towards a Partial Fusion of the International Covenants on Human Rights* 27 Osgood Hall LJ 769 (1989); *see also* Craig Scott, *Reaching Beyond (without abandoning) the Category of "Economic, Social and Cultural Rights"* 21 Hum. Rts. Q. 633, 643–650 (1999).

[91] The address was delivered to the 77th Congress on January 6, 1941, Congressional Record 1941, Vol. 87, Part I. *See also* <http://www.fdrlibrary.marist.edu/4free.html>.

[92] For an in-depth discussion of this concept, *see* Philip Alston & Gerard Quinn, *supra* n. 73, at 172–181. The authors opine, "The concept of progressive achievement is in many ways the linch-

are often perceived as "goals" or "objectives" rather than "true individual rights." The progressive realization of the rights under the ICESCR should be distinguished from the rights under the ICCPR, which embodies an immediate obligation to respect and ensure all of the relevant rights specified therein. This distinction is based on the wording of Article 2 of both the ICESCR and the ICCPR. Article 2 of the ICESCR obliges each State Party to take steps to the maximum of its available resources to achieve progressively the full realization of the rights under the ICESCR.[93] By contrast, Article 2 of the ICCPR obliges each State Party to respect and to ensure to all individuals within its territory and subject to its jurisdiction the rights recognized in the ICCPR.[94]

The difference between the two sets of rights has traditionally been perceived to be significant, and the distinction between the provisions of the ICESCR and the ICCPR remains important. That distinction is nowhere more evident than in

---

pin of the whole Covenant. Upon its meaning turns the nature of states obligations. Most of the rights granted depend in varying degrees on the availability of resources and this fact is recognized and reflected in the concept of 'progressive achievement'." *See also Core Obligations: Building a Framework for Economic, Social and Cultural Rights*, 4–5 (Audrey Chapman & Sage Russell, eds., Intersentia 2002), which discusses how the notion of "progressive realization" has complicated both the conceptualization and monitoring of economic, social, and cultural rights.

[93] Article 2 of ICESCR states:

"1. Each State party to the present Covenant undertakes to take steps, individually and through international assistance and co-operation, especially economic and technical, to the maximum of its available resources, with a view to achieving progressively the full realization of the rights recognized in the present Covenant by all appropriate means, including particularly the adoption of legislative measures.

2. The States Parties to the present Covenant undertake to guarantee that the rights enunciated in the present Covenant will be exercised without discrimination of any kind as to race, colour, sex, language, religion, political or other opinion, national or social origin, property, birth or other status.

3. Developing countries, with due regard to human rights and their national economy, may determine to what extent they would guarantee the economic rights recognized in the present Covenant to non-nationals."

In this connection, *see* General Comment No. 3 on the Nature of the States Parties' obligations under Article 2 of the ICESCR, *infra* n. 179 and n. 193. It is worth mentioning here that although the term "resources" in Article 2 (1) above is not defined, it is generally understood to refer to both financial and natural resources.

[94] Article 2 of the ICCPR states that

"1. Each State party to the present Covenant undertakes to respect and to ensure to all individuals within its territory and subject to its jurisdiction the rights recognized in the present Covenant, without distinction of any kind, such as race, colour, sex, language, religion, political or other opinion, national or social origin, property, birth or other status.

2. Where not already provided for by existing legislative or other measures, each State party to the present Covenant undertakes to take the necessary steps, in accordance with

the institutional structures pertaining to each. This section of the Study is devoted to understanding the implementation mechanisms of the two Covenants, and the evolution of the Committee on Economic, Social and Cultural Rights, in order to better understand the content of the rights under the ICESCR, and the nature of the import of General Comment No.15.

The history and institutional apparatus of the ICESCR is inextricably linked to the concept of "progressive realization" at the heart of the ICESCR's implementation. Describing "the two conceptions of implementation" discussed during the drafting of the two Covenants, Alston notes:

> The first was described as "critical, sanctional, censorial or negative" and was designed to assess "how far the situation in a given country fell short of what was required." The second, by contrast, was "constructive, helpful and cooperative" and sought to identify "methods of bringing actual conditions nearer to the ideal." There was virtually unanimous agreement that the latter was the appropriate model for the Economic and Social Council to follow in the case of economic, social and cultural rights.[95]

The core and exclusive reliance on the reporting mechanism as a means of implementation is also closely linked to the implementation of a set of rights that were not conceived as immediately realizable. It is contended also that part of why the evolution of the Committee has been so prolonged, is directly related to the conception of rights under the ICESCR as vague and aspirational,[96] rather than "true" justiciable, legal rights. Similarly, the obligations these rights entail

---

its constitutional processes and with the provisions of the present Covenant, to adopt such legislative or other measures as may be necessary to give effect to the rights recognized in the present Covenant.

3. Each State party to the present Covenant undertakes: (a) To ensure that any person whose rights or freedoms as herein recognized are violated shall have an effective remedy, notwithstanding that the violation has been committed by persons acting in an official capacity; (b) To ensure that any person claiming such a remedy shall have his right thereto determined by competent judicial, administrative or legislative authorities, or by any other competent authority provided for by the legal system of the State, and to develop the possibilities of judicial remedy; (c) To ensure that the competent authorities shall enforce such remedies when granted."

[95] Philip Alston, *Out of the Abyss: The Challenges Confronting the New UN Committee on Economic, Social, and Cultural Rights,* 9 Hum. Rts. Q. 332, 359 (1987). In this connection, *see* discussion of the concept of "progressive realization," *infra* n. 196.

[96] Matthew Craven, *supra.* n. 73 at 92.

have been characterized as "programmatic and promotional"[97] rather than immediate and absolute.[98]

A comprehensive analysis of the institutional history of each of the entities under the ICCPR and the ICESCR lies beyond the scope of this Study, but a brief comparative overview is appropriate, and indeed necessary. The Human Rights Committee was established under Article 28[99] of the ICCPR in 1976 at the first meeting of the States Parties to the ICCPR, shortly after the ICCPR entered into force.[100] It is composed of 18 human rights experts nominated by

---

[97] Ian Brownlie, *Principles of Public International Law*, 576 (5th ed., Oxford University Press 1998). Brownlie notes also the one exception to this, in Article 8 of the ICESCR on provisions relating to trade unions.

[98] For an early critique of the nature of rights contained in the ICESCR, *see* E.W. Vierdag, *The Legal Nature of Rights Granted by the International Covenant on Economic, Social and Cultural Rights*, 9 Netherlands Yearbook of International Law 69 (1978). For a strong exposition of the opposite view, *see* Godfried van Hoof, *The Legal Nature of Economic, Social and Cultural Rights: A Rebuttal of Some Traditional Views* in *The Right to Food*, 97–110 (Philip Alston & Katarina Tomaševski, eds., Martinus Nijhoff Publishers 1984).

[99] Article 28 of the ICCPR states:

"1. There shall be established a Human Rights Committee (hereafter referred to in the present Covenant as the Committee). It shall consist of eighteen members and shall carry out the functions hereinafter provided.

2. The Committee shall be composed of nationals of the States Parties to the present Covenant who shall be persons of high moral character and recognized competence in the field of human rights, consideration being given to the usefulness of the participation of some persons having legal experience.

3. The members of the Committee shall be elected and shall serve in their personal capacity."

The Secretary-General convened the first meeting of the States Parties on September 20, 1976 (U.N. Doc. CCPR/SP/7 (1976): decisions of the first meeting of the States Parties to the ICCPR.) Subsequent elections have taken place every two years, starting in 1978, for half the members of the Committee, as according to Article 32, the term of nine of the members elected at the first meeting expired at the end of two years. Although the 18 members are elected by the States Parties, they serve, as stated in Article 28 (3), in their personal capacity.

[100] The Human Rights Committee established under the ICCPR should be distinguished from the Commission on Human Rights established in 1946 by ECOSOC; *see supra* n. 57. It is the work of the Commission on Human Rights that resulted in the adoption of the ICCPR, and the establishment of the Human Rights Committee under the ICCPR. Reference should also be made in this connection to the office of the United Nations High Commissioner for Human Rights. The recommendation for the establishment of the post of United Nations High Commissioner for Human Rights emanated from the World Conference on Human Rights that was held in Vienna in June 1993 (*see supra* n. 66). Paragraph 18 of the Programme of Action accompanying the Vienna Declaration recommended to the General Assembly, when examining the report of the Conference at its forty-eighth session that, "it begins, as a matter of priority, consideration of the question of the establishment of a High Commissioner for Human Rights for the promotion and protection of all human rights." The General Assembly of the

the States Parties of which they are nationals,[101] and elected by a secret ballot of all the States Parties, to serve a four-year term.[102] The primary functions of the Human Rights Committee, as set forth in the ICCPR and its first Optional Protocol, include conducting dialogue with the States Parties and drawing conclusions from their reports,[103] hearing interstate complaints under Article 41 of the ICCPR,[104] and issuing decisions on communications by individuals under the first Optional Protocol to the ICCPR.[105] The Committee also has, in connection with the mandatory reporting system under Article 40 of the ICCPR, the author-

---

United Nations accepted this recommendation and established, on December 20, 1993, the post of the United Nations High Commissioner for Human Rights (*see* General Assembly Resolution A/Res/48/141, 85th Plenary Meeting, December 20, 1993). The High Commissioner is appointed by the Secretary-General of the United Nations and approved by the General Assembly for a term of four years, with the possibility of one renewal for another fixed term of four years. The Resolution lays down in detail the responsibilities of the High Commissioner, which are based on the promotion and protection of the effective enjoyment by all of all civil, cultural, economic, political, and social rights, and include carrying out tasks assigned by the competent bodies of the United Nations system in the field of human rights, as well as making recommendations thereon with the view to improving the promotion and protection of human rights. The responsibilities also include overall supervision of the Centre for Human Rights (*see supra* n. 57). The High Commissioner is based in Geneva, with a liaison office in New York, and reports annually to the Commission on Human Rights and, through the Economic and Social Council, to the General Assembly of the United Nations. For more details on the United Nations High Commissioner for Human Rights, *see* <http://www.unhchr.ch>. *See also* Bertrand Ramcharan, *supra* n. 54, and n. 57.

[101] Article 29 of the ICCPR. Article 31 states that the Committee may not include more than one national of the same state.

[102] Article 32 of the ICCPR. Article 31 states that in the election of the Committee, consideration shall be given to equitable geographical distribution of membership and to the representation of the different forms of civilization and of the principal legal systems.

[103] These are the reports submitted to the Committee under the mandatory reporting system required under Article 40 of the ICCPR, which provides for the "consideration" and "study" of the national reports by the Committee. They are discussed in more detail later; *see infra* n. 106.

[104] Article 41 of the ICCPR deals with the recognition of the competence of the Human Rights Committee to receive and consider communications from one State Party against another State Party, claiming violations of the provisions of the ICCPR. For more details on this Article, how it operates, and its relationship with the rest of the provisions of the ICCPR, *see infra* n. 173.

[105] These functions are set forth in the ICCPR (Article 28, *supra* n. 99), and the first Optional Protocol to the ICCPR, which lays down the substantive procedures for the effective observance of the rights under the ICCPR. For discussion of the functions of the Human Rights Committee, *see* Dominic McGoldrick, *The Human Rights Committee: Its Role in the Development of the International Covenant on Civil and Political Rights* 50 (Clarendon Press 1991). There are two optional protocols to the ICCPR. The first Optional Protocol was adopted by General Assembly Resolution 2200A (XXI) of December 16, 1966, opened for signature thereafter, and entered into force on March 23, 1976, in accordance with Article 9. *See* 21 U.N. GAOR Supp. (No. 16) at 59, U.N. Doc. A/6316 (1966), 999 U.N.T.S. 302. It is worth noting that the Protocol entered into force the same day the ICCPR itself entered into

ity to issue general comments, as specified under Article 40 (4).[106] In addition to these more substantive aspects of its work, the Committee is required to submit to the General Assembly, through the ECOSOC, an annual report on its activities under Article 45 of the ICCPR.[107]

By contrast, the Committee on Economic, Social and Cultural Rights was established by ECOSOC rather than emanating directly from a specific provision of the ICESCR. Another important distinction to draw between the two bodies is that the Human Rights Committee was established immediately after the ICCPR entered into force in 1976, while the Committee on Economic, Social and Cultural Rights evolved gradually through a number of ECOSOC resolutions and decisions, and emerged in its current structure in 1985, nine years after the ICESCR entered into force in 1976.

---

force. The Protocol recognizes the authority of the Human Rights Committee to receive and consider communications from individuals claiming violations of the provisions of the ICCPR by a State party. The Second Optional Protocol to the ICCPR aims at the abolition of the death penalty. *See* Second Optional Protocol to the International Covenant on Civil and Political Rights, Aiming at the Abolition of the Death Penalty, G.A. res. 44/128 of December 15, 1989; annex, 44 U.N. GAOR Supp. (No. 49) at 207, U.N. Doc. A/44/49 (1989), 1642 U.N.T.S. 414, entered into force July 11, 1991.

[106] Article 40 (4) of the ICCPR states that "The Committee shall study the reports submitted by the States Parties to the Present Covenant. It shall transmit its reports, and such general comments as it may consider appropriate, to the States Parties. The Committee may also transmit to the Economic and Social Council these comments along with the copies of the reports it has received from States Parties to the present Covenant." Between 1981 and 2002 the Human Rights Committee has issued 30 General Comments ranging from the Right to Life (General Comment No. 6: Article 6: The Right to Life, A/37/40 (1982) 93), Peoples' Right to Self-Determination (ICCPR General Comment No. 12— Twenty-first session, 1984): Article 1: The Right to Self-Determination of Peoples, A/39/40 (1984) 142); the Right to Privacy (General Comment No.16 (Thirty-second session, 1988)): Article 17: The Right to Respect of Privacy, Family, Home and Correspondence, and Protection of Honour and Reputation, A/43/40 (1988) 181); and the Right of Non-Discrimination (General Comment No.18 (Thirty-seventh session, 1989)): Non-Discrimination, A/45/40 vol. I (1990) 173). Other, more recent General Comments have addressed the Right to Freedom of Movement (General Comment 27 (Sixty-seventh session, 1999)): Article 12: Freedom of Movement, A/55/40 vol. I (2000) 128; and the Right of Equality of Rights between Men and Women (General Comment No. 28 (Sixty-eighth session, 2000)): Article 3: Equality of Rights Between Men and Women, A/55/40 vol. I (2000) 133). For a detailed discussion of the General Comments issued by the Human Rights Committee *see* <http://www1.umn.edu/humanrts/gencomm/econ.htm>. Article 40 (5) of the ICCPR gives the States Parties the right to "submit to the Committee observations on any comments that may be made in accordance with paragraph 4 of this article."

[107] Article 45 of the ICCPR states that "The Committee shall submit to the General Assembly of the United Nations, through the Economic and Social Council, an annual report on its activities." Another initiative worth noting is the Committee's adoption, in April 1987, of a "Statement on the Second Decade to Combat Racism and Racial Discrimination" (SR 725; Doc.A/42/40, pr.18). It should also be noted, however, that no explicit provision exists giving the Committee jurisdiction to issue such statements.

ECOSOC had, as early as 1976,[108] considered and adopted a Resolution[109] that set forth procedures that would be required for the implementation of the ICESCR, having explicitly recognized the important responsibilities placed on the ECOSOC by the ICESCR. The Resolution established a program under which the States Parties to the ICESCR would furnish to ECOSOC, in biennial stages, the reports referred to in Article 16 of the ICESCR.[110] The Resolution invited the States Parties to submit to the Secretary-General, in conformity with Part IV of the ICESCR and the program referred to above, reports on the measures that they adopted and the progress made in achieving the observance of the rights recognized under the ICESCR.[111] Furthermore, the Resolution required the States Parties to indicate, when necessary, factors and difficulties affecting the degree of their fulfillment of their obligation under the ICESCR.[112]

The first body to oversee ECOSOC's responsibilities under the ICESCR was established in 1978. In that year ECOSOC adopted a Decision[113] creating

> a sessional working group on the implementation of the International Covenant on Economic, Social and Cultural Rights, composed of 15 members of the Council which are also States parties to the Covenant: 3 members from African States, 3 members from Asian States, 3 members from Eastern European States, 3 members from Latin American States and 3 members from Western Europe and other States; . . .[114]

---

[108] The ICESCR entered into force on January 3, 1976, in accordance with its Article 27; *see also* General Assembly Resolution 2200 A (XXI) of December 16, 1966.

[109] ECOSOC Resolution 1988 (LX): Procedures for the implementation of the International Covenant on Economic, Social and Cultural Rights of May 11, 1976 (1,999th Plenary Meeting). Paragraph 9 (a) provides that "A sessional working group of the Economic and Social Council, with appropriate representation of States Parties to the Covenant, and with due regard to the equitable geographical distribution, shall be established by the Council whenever reports are due for consideration by the Council, for the purposes of assisting it in the consideration of such reports." The Resolution posits the self-reporting requirement at the heart of the monitoring process, and as the primary focus of the new Sessional Group's work.

[110] *See id.*, paragraph 1. The Paragraph sets forth three stages. The First Stage dealt with the rights covered by Articles 6–9, the Second Stage with Articles 10–12, and the Third Stage with Articles 13–15.

[111] *See id.*, paragraph 3. Part IV of the ICESCR deals with the reports to be submitted to ECOSOC.

[112] *See id.*

[113] ECOSOC Decision E/1978/10 of May 3, 1978: Composition of the Sessional working group on the implementation of the International Covenant on Economic, Social and Cultural Rights.

[114] *See id.*, paragraph (a).

The purpose of the Working Group was to assist ECOSOC in consideration of the reports submitted by the States Parties to the ICESCR.[115]

In 1981, the Working Group was renamed the "Sessional Working Group of Governmental Experts on the Implementation of the International Covenant on Economic, Social and Cultural Rights."[116]

However, the difficulties faced by the Working Group in its early years in discharging its responsibilities[117] led to the increased formalization of its composition, organization, and administrative arrangements in 1982.[118] In that year, the Council adopted the Resolution renaming the Group as the "Sessional Working Group of Governmental Experts on the Implementation of the International Covenant on Economic, Social and Cultural Rights (hereinafter referred to as 'the Group of Experts')."[119] The Group of Experts consisted of 15 members elected by ECOSOC for a term of three years with the possibility of reelection at the end of their terms.[120] The Group was required to submit to ECOSOC, at the end of each session, a report on the activities of the Group and any general suggestions and recommendations, based on its reports, that would assist the Committee in discharging its duties.[121]

The initial establishment of a body by ECOSOC to "assist" it in the "consideration of reports submitted by States Parties"[122] represented a significant move, and

---

[115] *See id.*

[116] ECOSOC Decision E/1981/158 of May 8, 1981: Review of the composition, organization, and administrative working arrangements of the Sessional Working Group on the Implementation of the International Covenant on Economic, Social and Cultural Rights, Paragraph 1. This Resolution did not change the number of members of the group, nor the criteria related to its composition (for example, equal distribution among geographical regions) or working methods. *See also* ECOSOC Resolution 1982/33 of May 6, 1982: Review of the composition, organization, and administrative working arrangements of the Sessional Working Group on the Implementation of the International Covenant on Economic, Social and Cultural Rights.

[117] Those difficulties were noted in Recital 4 of ECOSOC Resolution 1980/24 of May 2, 1980, which stated: "*Noting* that the Sessional Working Group, established under its decision 1978/10, encountered certain difficulties in discharging its responsibilities under the present arrangements." *See also* Philip Alston, *supra.* n. 95, at 340–349.

[118] ECOSOC Resolution 1982/33: Review of the composition, organization and administrative arrangements of the Sessional Working Group (of Governmental Experts) on the Implementation of the International Covenant on Economic, Social and Cultural Rights of 27th Plenary Meeting, May 6, 1982.

[119] *See id.*, paragraph (a). The only difference in the new name is that the Group was referred to as the Group of Experts.

[120] *See id.*, paragraph (b) (i).

[121] *See id.*, paragraph (d).

[122] In accordance with ECOSOC Decision 1978/10 of May 3, 1978.

perhaps an effort on ECOSOC's part to heighten the prominence of the ICESCR and provide it with a monitoring body akin to the Human Rights Committee operating under the ICCPR.[123] However, at its inception this Group remained very much a part of ECOSOC, rather than a body with its own independent identity. Indeed, in terms of composition, the guidelines were still fluid, and ECOSOC did not originally require any specific geographic representation, nor even that the members be internationally recognized experts in the field of human rights.[124]

However, by 1978, the formalization of the working methods of the new entity was becoming more evident,[125] and ECOSOC requested the Working Group to prepare for consideration by the Council recommendations on its methods of work in connection with the reports of the States Parties to the ICESCR.[126] The Group's recommendations were approved by ECOSOC in 1979, which saw the further formalization of its working methods, and an increasingly quasi-judicial function emerging.[127] Thus, for example, the 1979 ECOSOC Resolution saw the emergence of an entitlement of States Parties to be present at the meetings at which their reports were being considered, and to make statements on the reports submitted by their States, as well as to answer questions that may be put to them by the Working Group.[128] Further, the President of ECOSOC would have to notify the

---

[123] *See supra* n. 99.

[124] In paragraph 10 of Resolution 1988 (LX) of May 11, 1976, ECOSOC simply "Appeals to States to include, if possible, in its delegations to the relevant sessions of the Economic and Social Council, members competent in the subject matters under consideration."

[125] ECOSOC Decision 1978/9 of May 3, 1978: Preparation of documentation to facilitate the work of the sessional working group on the implementation of the International Covenant on Economic, Social and Cultural Rights and 1978/10 of May 3, 1978: Composition of the sessional working group on the implementation of the International Covenant on Economic, Social and Cultural Rights. Decision 1978/10 established the Group composed of 15 Council Members who are also States Parties to the ICESCR. Of note also was the Council's decision to review its decision at its first regular session in 1981 taking into account the principle of equitable geographical distribution and the increase in the number of States Parties to the ICESCR.

[126] ECOSOC Decision 1978 /10 of May 3, 1978, paragraph (d).

[127] That being said, Decision 1979/43 makes clear that the Working Group should endeavor to work on the basis of the principle of consensus. The increasing responsibility inherent in the Group's function was also evident in the introduction of the possibility of a general discussion being held on the measures adopted and the progress made in achieving the observance of the rights recognized under the ICESCR. Finally, the Resolution provides that the Sessional Group may send ECOSOC recommendations of a general nature referred to in Article 21 of the ICESCR, and that at each session, the Group should consider the status of reporting under Article 16 and make appropriate recommendations in its report to ECOSOC.

[128] ECOSOC Resolution 1979/43 of May 11, 1979 (18th Plenary Meeting), paragraph 7.

States Parties of the sessions at which their reports would be considered, and extend a special invitation to such States to attend sessions of this type.[129] The emergence of such procedural guidelines is significant in the context of the increased "judicialization" of the workings of this entity, and represented perhaps an early bid for institutional legitimacy. The 1981 ECOSOC Resolution[130] incorporated an understanding reached on the role and participation of the specialized agencies, allowing the latter to make general statements on matters related to their field of competence, and allowing the States Parties that presented reports to the Working Group to be free to respond to or to take into account the general comments made by the specialized agencies.[131] This would again place the Working Group in an adjudicative and supervisory role, making it *the forum* within which discussions of the implementation of the ICESCR would take place.

The final steps of the institutional evolution of the body responsible for the ICESCR were taken in 1985, through ECOSOC Resolution 1985/17.[132] This was indeed a milestone resolution with regard to the composition, organization, and functions of this body. The Resolution changed the name of the Group to the "Committee on Economic, Social and Cultural Rights."[133] Furthermore, it increased the number of its members to 18,[134] and determined that these would be experts with recognized competence in the field of human rights serving in their individual capacities. The Resolution stipulated that due consideration should be given to equitable geographical distribution and the representation of different forms of social and legal systems.[135] Those characteristics remain evident in the composition of the current Committee.[136]

---

[129] *See id.*, paragraph 8.

[130] ECOSOC Resolution 1981/158: Review of the composition, organization and administrative agreements of the Sessional Working Group on the Implementation of the International Covenant on Economic, Social and Cultural Rights, of May 8, 1981 (19th Plenary Meeting).

[131] *See id.*, paragraph 9.

[132] ECOSOC Resolution 1985/17: Review of the composition, organization and administrative arrangements of the Sessional Working Group of Governmental Experts on the Implementation of the International Covenant on Economic, Social and Cultural Rights, of May 28, 1985. *See also* appendix IV of this Study.

[133] *See id.*, paragraph (a).

[134] *See id.*, paragraph (b).

[135] *See id.*

[136] The Committee is composed of the following Experts: Mr. Clément Atangana (Cameroon),** Mrs. Rocío Barahona Riera (Costa Rica),* Mrs. Virginia Bonoan-Dandan (Philippines),** Mrs.

The Resolution stated further that the members of the Committee would be elected by secret ballot from a list of persons nominated by the States Parties to the ICESCR for a term of four years, with eligibility for reelection at the end of the term if renominated.[137] The increase in length of the term is also significant with respect to the judicialization of the body and its working methods. The ECOSOC Resolution required the Committee to submit to the ECOSOC a report on its activities, including a summary of its consideration of the reports submitted by the States Parties to the ICESCR.[138] This Resolution brought the work of the Committee on Economic, Social and Cultural Rights in line with that of the Human Rights Committee with regard to the receipt and consideration of reports from the States Parties, and the submission to ECOSOC of a report on their activities.[139] The Resolution further authorized the Committee to make suggestions and recommendations of a general nature on the basis of its consideration of those reports and the reports submitted by the U.N. specialized agencies. The purpose behind those suggestions and recommendations was to assist ECOSOC in fulfilling its responsibilities under Articles 21 and 22 of the ICESCR.[140]

Thus, through the 1985 ECOSOC Resolution, the Committee on Economic, Social and Cultural Rights gained equivalence with the Human Rights Committee, in terms of number of members, their election process and qualifications, and more importantly, in terms of functions and supervisory role for its respective Covenant.

By 1987 the Committee on Economic, Social and Cultural Rights was firmly in place, and its status confirmed, although its visibility and prominence still needed

---

Maria Virginia Bras Gomes (Portugal),** Mr. Dumitru Ceausu (Romania),* Mr. Abdessatar Grissa (Tunisia),* Mrs. Chokila Iyer (India),** Mr. Azzouz Kerdoun (Algeria),** Mr. Yuri Kolosov (Russian Federation),** Mr. Giorgio Malinverni (Switzerland),* Mr. Jaime Marchán Romero (Ecuador),** Mr. Sergei Martynov (Belarus),* Mr. Ariranga Govindasamy Pillay (Mauritius),* Mr. Kenneth Osborne Rattray (Jamaica),* Mr. Eibe Riedel (Germany),** Mr. Walid M. Sa'di (Jordan),* Mr. Philippe Texier (France),* and Mr. Alvaro Tirado Mejia (Colombia).** For the composition of the Committee, *see* UNGA A/58/100 (58th Session, June 13, 2003), at <http://domino.un.org/unispal.nsf/9a798adbf322aff38525617b006d88d7/16452a902148853585256e19005c380c/$FILE/a58_100.pdf> at 187.

Note: * Term of office expires on December 31, 2004. ** Term of office expires on December 31, 2006.

[137] *See supra,* n. 132, paragraph (c) (i).

[138] *See id.,* paragraph (f).

[139] *See* Article 40 of the ICCPR, *supra* n. 106.

[140] *See supra* n. 132, paragraph (f).

buttressing. In its Resolution 1987/5, ECOSOC reaffirmed the importance of increasing public awareness of the Committee and the role Non-governmental Organizations (NGOs) could play in that regard.[141] It also confirmed the role of NGOs in the implementation of the ICESCR. In particular, it invited them, in consultative status with ECOSOC, to submit written statements that might contribute to the full and universal recognition and realization of the rights contained in the ICESCR, and to make those statements available to the Committee in a timely manner.[142] Most importantly, Paragraph 7 of the Resolution "invited the Committee to consider again at its next session the compilation of recommendations in the summary records of the Committee relating to its future work, paying particular regard to practices followed by other treaty bodies, including the preparation of general comments by the Human Rights Committee." The invitation to consider the compilation of recommendations, ". . . paying particular attention to the practice followed by other treaty bodies, including the preparation of general comments by the Human Rights Committee," was subsequently endorsed by the General Assembly of the United Nations.[143] Paragraph 7 of the United Nations General Assembly Resolution accorded some parity to the status of the Human Rights Committee, and the Committee on Economic, Social and Cultural Rights when it urged the Secretary-General of the United Nations "to take determined steps, within existing resources, to give publicity to the Human Rights Committee and to the Committee on Economic, Social and Cultural Rights and to ensure that they receive full administrative support in order to enable them to discharge their functions effectively."

In its 1992 report, the Committee would reemphasize in unequivocal terms the critical role played by NGOs in the process of information gathering and ultimately, in the implementation of the ICESCR.[144] In this, it would further strengthen its fact-finding and investigative role, and again, reinforce the Committee's position as the central "quasi-judicial" authority of the ICESCR.

---

[141] ECOSOC Resolution 1987/5: International Covenant on Economic, Social and Cultural Rights 14th Plenary Meeting, May 26, 1987.

[142] *See id.*, paragraph 6.

[143] *See* General Assembly Resolution A/Res/42/102, *supra* n. 81, paragraph 5. That provision of the Resolution went further and affirmed the relevance and importance of the reports submitted by the States Parties to the Covenants to the two Committees.

[144] Committee on Economic, Social and Cultural Rights (Report of the Sixth Session E/1992/23) Supplement No. 3, paragraphs 384–6. *See also* Philip Alston, *supra*, n. 95, at 367–374.

Among the efforts to formalize and make the work of the Committee more judicial and less political were important initiatives regarding its working methods. As discussed earlier, ECOSOC Resolution 1987/5 invited the Committee to consider the compilation of recommendations in its summary records relating to future work "paying particular regard to practices followed by other treaty bodies, including the preparation of general comments by the Human Rights Committee."[145] The Committee followed up on this suggestion. During the course of its sixth session, after considering the most constructive way of approaching the evolving practice of issuing concluding comments, the Committee issued a set of guidelines or criteria that would frame its approach. These guidelines concentrated almost exclusively on the reporting procedure and the ensuing process of questions and answers.[146] The Committee would again address those guidelines, and determine that it was necessary that they be broadened, so as to "focus not only on the extent to which the report and the other information provided (both orally and in writing) were satisfactory or not, but also on the extent to which the situation in the country concerned in terms of the realization of the rights contained in the ICESCR was satisfactory."[147]

The Committee's role, as the central entity for the ICESCR, with the power to issue definitive and authoritative statements on the nature and realization of the rights set forth in the ICESCR was clearly consolidated. With deliberate reference made to the practice of other established Treaty bodies,[148] the Committee ". . . decided that it would adopt, at the end of its consideration of each report, concluding observations reflecting the main points of discussion and indicating issues that would require a specific follow-up. Those concluding observations would serve as a starting point for the periodic reports to be submitted by States

---

[145] *See supra* n. 141, paragraph 9.

[146] Committee on Economic, Social and Cultural Rights (Report of the Sixth Session E/1992/23) Supplement No. 3, paragraph 383.

[147] Committee on Economic, Social and Cultural Rights (Report of the Seventh Session E/1993/22) Supplement No. 2, paragraph 263. The Committee's concluding observations would follow a common structure, including an introduction of a general nature, a section on progress achieved, another on factors and difficulties impeding the application of the Covenant, one on the principal subjects of concern, and a final one including suggestions and recommendations addressed to the State Party.

[148] *See id.*, paragraphs 264 and 265. The Committee observed that the practice of concluding comments was one being adopted by other treaty bodies, and also noted the desirability of a more coordinated approach, where appropriate.

Parties at a later stage."[149] The latter two developments may have been among the most significant in terms of establishing and strengthening the quasi-judicial nature and role of the Committee. Its investigative role confirmed, it was now reaching boldly into the realm of asserting its authority to judge the relative performance of the States Parties with respect to their obligations under the ICESCR.

Concurrent with the new endorsement of its adjudicative role, and referring to "other treaty bodies including the Human Rights Committee," the Committee went on to highlight "the importance of providing the State Party, following the *examination* of the report, with an *authoritative statement* conveying the views of the Committee on the implementation of the Covenant by that State party" (emphasis added).[150]

A number of very important developments, of direct relevance to the weight of General Comment No.15, can be identified in the institutional evolution traced above.

First, there was a very clear increase in the level of responsibilities with which the body responsible for the implementation of the ICESCR was entrusted. In this, the Committee on Economic, Social and Cultural Rights was now resembling more and more the Human Rights Committee responsible for the ICCPR. It is interesting to postulate how this gradually evolving parity in the independence and status of the two bodies contributes to a greater balance of influence between them, between the two Covenants, and ultimately between the two sets of rights under them, all of which are concurrent with the repeated endorsements of the interdependence and equality of all human rights. This parity is clearly manifest in the United Nations General Assembly Resolution discussed above.

Second, and connected with this increase in responsibility, is the enhanced diversity of the Committee's tasks. It was no longer confined to "assisting" ECOSOC, but was now adding to that portfolio the tasks of investigation, fact-finding, and judgment as to the implementation of the rights under the ICESCR, and the administrative law functions of hearings and receiving reports and submissions by parties.

---

[149] Committee on Economic, Social and Cultural Rights (Report of the Seventh Session E/1993/22) Supplement No. 2, paragraph 264.

[150] *See id.*, paragraph 265.

A third development was the gradual "depoliticization" of the body and its increasing independence,[151] with its members no longer designated by the States Parties' Governments to the ICESCR, but rather elected by ECOSOC. Greater emphasis would now be placed on the expertise and independence of these members, who would serve in their personal capacity rather than as representatives of their Governments, and who would report to ECOSOC.

Connected with this was the increasingly formalized adjudicative or quasi-judicial role being carved out for the body. By 1985, the active role of the Committee as a quasi-judicial body became clear,[152] despite the continued absence of any mechanism in place for individual communications or petitions.[153] Furthermore, the term that Committee members would serve was gradually extended to four years, with the possibility of renewal, which would also enhance the "quasi-judicial" nature of the Committee's function and vest the Committee members' work with greater continuity and stability.

These aspects of the quasi-judicial or administrative law role of the reporting system can also be seen as "law-making," in the way a court makes law through the adjudication of cases. However, by far the most significant source of interpretative law remains the General Comments, which will be explored in greater detail in the next Part. At this juncture, however, it is worth noting that the emergence of these practices has occurred together, in a mutually reinforcing way, consolidating the ever more prominent and assertive stance of the Committee as *the* adjudicative body of the ICESCR. As Alston notes, "The [reporting] process is a continuing one with ramifications that go considerably beyond the inevitably

---

[151] For an insightful analysis of the history of the Committee and the relevant *travaux préparatoires,* as well as an examination of the evolution of the Committee from being a highly politicized entity to the independent body it is today, *see* Philip Alston, *supra* n. 95, at 335–349.

[152] Matthew Craven, *supra* n. 73, at 91.

[153] While to date there are no Optional Protocols to the ICESCR, proposals for a petition system under the ICESCR have been discussed on a number of occasions. At its sixth session, in 1991, the Committee supported the drafting of an optional protocol "since that would enhance the practical implementation of the Covenant as well as the dialogue with States Parties and would make it possible to focus the attention of public opinion to a greater extent on economic, social and cultural rights." A resolution (Commission on Human Rights Resolution 2002/24) on economic, social, and cultural rights adopted by the 58th session of the Commission on Human Rights included several references to the need to elaborate an optional protocol to the ICESCR. On the issue of a proposed Protocol to the ICESCR, *see* generally, Philip Alston, *Establishing a right to petition under the Covenant on Economic, Social and Cultural*

formalistic procedure of the Committee itself."[154] It is also worth noting in this connection that, to date, no objection has been raised by any State Party to either practice. This is perhaps a reflection of the endorsement contained in the General Assembly Resolution related to the Committee's work and to the preparation of general comments.[155]

The developments noted above regarding the evolution of the Committee on Economic, Social and Cultural Rights, and the gradual "maturing" of its working methods, bestow both the concluding observations and General Comments issued by the Committee with a significant measure of legitimacy, and arguably cloak at least the latter with the authority of "law."[156]

Rights, in *Collected Courses of the Academy of European Law: The Protection of Human Rights in Europe* Vol. IV, Book 2, 115 (Philip Alston & Bruno de Witte, eds., European University Institute 1993); *The Right to Complain about Economic, Social and Cultural Rights: Proceedings of the Expert Meeting on the Adoption of an Optional Protocol to the International Covenant on Economic, Social and Cultural Rights* (Utrecht, January 25–28, 1995) (F. Coomans & G. J. H. van Hoof, eds., Netherlands Institute of Human Rights 1995); Matthew Craven, *Towards an unofficial petition procedure: A review of the role of the UN Committee on Economic, Social and Cultural Rights* in *Social Rights as Human Rights: A European Challenge,* 91 (Krzysztof Drzewicki, Catarina Krause and Allan Rosas, eds., Abo/Turku (Finland), Abo Akademi University, Institute for Human Rights 1994). As discussed earlier, *supra* n. 105, there are two optional protocols to the ICCPR. Parties to the first Optional Protocol to the International Covenant on Civil and Political Rights recognize the authority of the Human Rights Committee to receive and consider communications from individuals claiming violations of the provisions of the ICCPR by a State Party. The Second Optional Protocol under the ICCPR concerns the abolition of the death penalty. *See* Second Optional Protocol to the International Covenant on Civil and Political Rights, aiming at the abolition of the death penalty, *supra* n. 105.

[154] Philip Alston, *supra* n. 95.

[155] *See supra* n. 143. *See also* Matthew Craven, *supra* n. 73, at 90, on no objection having been made to the practice of General Comments.

[156] Joseph Raz, *The Authority of Law: Essays on Law and Morality* (Oxford University Press 1979); Herbert L. A. Hart, *The Concept of Law* (2d ed., Oxford University Press 1994).

PART THREE
General Comments Issued by the Committee on Economic, Social and Cultural Rights

Evolution of the Role of the Committee and Its Early Comments

A major challenge facing both Covenants is norm clarification. That is particularly true of the ICESCR. As Alston noted in regard to the ICESCR in 1987, "one of the most striking features of the Covenant is the vagueness of the normative implications of the various rights it contains."[157] Alston also noted the compounding factors of the dearth of domestic jurisprudence on such rights, and "the failure of the international community to develop jurisprudence of any significance on many of the principal economic rights since the Covenant's adoption in 1966."[158] The innovation of General Comments is therefore particularly relevant in regard to the ICESCR.

As discussed in the preceding Part of this Study, it would take almost 10 years after the ICESCR's entry into force for the Committee on Economic, Social and Cultural Rights to take its current form. As the previous discussion illustrates, ECOSOC Resolution 1985/17 would complete the evolution of the Working Group into a Committee. However, it was only in 1987 that ECOSOC invited the Committee to consider the preparation of general comments in a manner akin to the practice followed by the Human Rights Committee. As the previous discussion also highlighted, that invitation was subsequently endorsed by the United Nations General Assembly.

In 1988, following that invitation, the Committee on Economic, Social and Cultural Rights formally undertook the preparation of "General Comments" on the various articles and provisions of the ICESCR.[159] This practice would be

---

[157] Philip Alston, *supra* n. 95, at 351.

[158] *See id.*

[159] Committee on Economic, Social and Cultural Rights, Report of the Second Session, U.N. Doc. E/1988/14, paragraphs 366 and 367. *See also supra* n. 141, paragraph 9.

rooted in, and derive its implied authority from, the ICESCR provisions on reporting, and its mandate to assist ECOSOC in the consideration of the Reports submitted by the States Parties under Articles 16 and 17 of the ICESCR.[160]

Practically, General Comments are adopted by the Committee in the following way: Any member of the Committee may put forward a draft general comment for consideration by the Committee in plenary. If adopted by the Committee, it is included in the Committee's annual report to ECOSOC and brought to the attention of the General Assembly, which also transmits the text to States Parties to the ICESCR. Comments by the States Parties or the specialized agencies in response to the General Comments are required to be brought to the attention of the Committee at its next session.[161]

The purpose of these General Comments provided further evidence of a body in an increasingly active quasi-judicial role. In its own words:

> The Committee endeavours, through its general comments, to make the experience gained so far through the examination of these reports available for the benefit of all States Parties in order to assist and promote their further implementation of the Covenant; to draw the attention of the States Parties to insufficiencies disclosed by a large number of reports; to suggest improvements in the reporting procedures and to stimulate the activities of the States Parties, the international organizations and the specialized agencies concerned in achieving progressively and effectively the full realization of the rights recognized in the Covenant. Whenever necessary, the Committee may, in the light of the experience of States Parties and of the conclusions which it has drawn therefrom, revise and update its general comments.[162]

---

[160] Craven notes that it is unclear as to whether the power of the Committee to make General Comments could be implied by the terms of the Covenant, but he also notes that no states have objected to such an interpretation. *See* Matthew Craven, *supra* n. 73, at 89–90. Article 17 (1) of the ICESCR states that "The States Parties to the present Covenant shall furnish their reports in stages, in accordance with a programme to be established by the Economic and Social Council within one year of the entry into force of the present Covenant after consultation with the States Parties and the specialized agencies concerned."

[161] This process was established by the Committee at its Second Session in 1988. *See* Report of the Committee on Economic, Social and Cultural Rights, Second Session, U.N. Doc. E/1988/14, paragraph 370.

[162] Introduction to the Committee's 1989 report to the Economic and Social Council E/1989/22, paragraph 3. The reference in the above quoted paragraph to "these reports" refers to the reports specified in Article 16 of the ICESCR. That Article states that "(1) The States

A number of aspects of this 1989 clarification are worthy of note. First, the practice of General Comments remains rooted in the reporting system, and in the Committee's role in assisting the States Parties to fulfill their reporting obligations. But the new practice goes further, casting the Committee in a role of judgment in which it can draw attention to insufficiencies disclosed in the report. It is worth noting here, in respect of the models of implementation discussed above, that this new practice brings the ICESCR model of implementation away from the originally conceived constructive model, and closer to the sanctional model traditionally associated with the ICCPR. Of significance also is the power assigned to the Committee to encourage *action* in suggesting improvements in reporting or by stimulating activities by Parties and international organizations. One final innovation is the possibility for revision and updating of the General Comments, which vests them with the appearance of legislative or administrative measures, and

---

Parties to the present Covenant undertake to submit in conformity with this part of the Covenant reports on the measures which they have adopted and the progress made in achieving the observance of the rights recognized therein." Section 2 (a) of this Article clarifies that such reports shall be submitted to the Secretary-General of the United Nations who shall transmit copies to ECOSOC for consideration in accordance with the provisions of the ICESCR. Section 2 (b) authorizes the Secretary-General to submit to the specialized agencies copies of those reports, or any relevant parts therefrom, from States Parties to the ICESCR that are also members of these specialized agencies, insofar as these reports, or any parts therefrom, relate to any matters that fall within the responsibilities of the said agencies in accordance with their constitutional instruments. Similarly, the ICCPR contains a compulsory monitoring system under Article 40, which provides:

"1. The States Parties to the present Covenant undertake to submit reports on the measures they have adopted which give effect to the rights recognized herein and on the progress made in the enjoyment of those rights:

(a) Within one year of the entry into force of the present Covenant for the States Parties concerned;

(b) Thereafter whenever the Committee so requests.

2. All reports shall be submitted to the Secretary-General of the United Nations, who shall transmit them to the Committee for consideration. Reports shall indicate the factors and difficulties, if any, affecting the implementation of the present Covenant.

3. The Secretary-General of the United Nations may, after consultation with the Committee, transmit to the specialized agencies concerned copies of such parts of the reports as may fall within their field of competence.

4. The Committee shall study the reports submitted by the States Parties to the present Covenant. It shall transmit its reports, and such general comments as it may consider appropriate, to the States Parties. The Committee may also transmit to the Economic and Social Council these comments along with the copies of the reports it has received from States Parties to the present Covenant.

5. The States Parties to the present Covenant may submit to the Committee observations on any comments that may be made in accordance with paragraph 4 of this article."

which are envisaged to guide States Parties, remain "in force" for significant periods of time, and remain relevant by being kept up to date by the Committee in light of the experience of States Parties and the conclusions it would draw from that.

At its Twenty-first session in 1999, the Committee adopted an Outline it would follow in drafting General Comments, entitled "Implementation of the International Covenant on Economic, Social and Cultural Rights (ICESCR)."[163] The Outline is useful for a number of reasons. It not only offers a measure of clarity to the form and content of General Comments, but it also provides further insight into the purpose it is intended to fulfill, particularly in the context of an instrument embodying rights that are subject to "progressive realization" and one in which enforcement has historically been weak. The Outline also offers further evidence of the incipient adjudicative function discussed above, being embraced by a now more confident Committee, aware of its stature and the authority of its pronouncements.

This Outline posits the role of General Comments as historic, descriptive, and normative. That is, they are intended to set forth in comprehensive and in-depth terms the genesis of the right, grounding this in its basic premises and principles, in its *travaux préparatoires* or drafting history.[164] The analysis is also descriptive and comparative, looking at the right in the broader international law context, against the backdrop of provisions in global or regional human rights instruments, other General Comments and the relevant documents of the Committee on Economic, Social and Cultural Rights. General Comments are, of course, in significant part, normative instruments, and the 1999 Outline makes this explicit, devoting an entire section to the "normative contents of the right"[165] in which the core content, elements of the right other than the core content, and justiciable aspects of the right are explored.

Finally, and most significantly for the emergence of a quasi-judicial body in the Committee, and a quasi-judicial process in the General Comments as an alternative to an "Optional Protocol Petition system," is the analysis of a "State party's obligations"[166] on the basis of the following categorizations: entitlements ensu-

---

[163] The Outline was adopted by the Committee on Economic, Social and Cultural Rights at its Twenty-first session, November 15–December 3, 1999. *See* <http://www.unhchr.ch/html/menu2/6/cescrnote.htm#outline>.

[164] For this, the Outline cites relevant records of the Commission on Human Rights, ECOSOC, and the General Assembly during the drafting of the Covenant. *See* Part I of the Outline.

[165] Part II of the Outline.

[166] Part III of the Outline.

ing from the right, and justiciable aspects of the right. The first of these is obviously the most important feature for the purposes of the right to water.

The Outline stipulates that a State Party's obligations[167] will also be determined, and recommendations made, in respect of what the Committee categorizes as obligations of immediacy and of progressive realization; obligations of conduct and obligations of result; and obligations to respect, to protect, and to fulfill; and obligations to promote. In addition to those "affirmative" obligations, the Outline stipulates that violations must also be considered, which include violations ensuing from acts of commission or omission, violations related to elements of the minimum core content of the right, and discrimination. In addition to this, General Comments should include analysis of noncompliance for reasons within the State's control, and retrogressive measures. Beyond this, the Committee may issue recommendations for States Parties with respect to the legal, administrative, and judicial framework;[168] monitoring obligations at the national level; reporting obligations; and national plans of action or State policies and directives; as well as the use of indicators and setting of national benchmarks.[169]

General Comments themselves are not binding *per se* because the Committee on Economic, Social and Cultural Rights does not have authority to create new obligations for the States Parties to the ICESCR. However, those Comments, as Craven noted, carry significant legal weight.[170] This is due in large part to the absence of any other authoritative body or procedure for settling interpretative questions related to the ICESCR.[171] The legal weight of the General Comments can also be attributed to the manner in which the body responsible for the ICESCR has evolved and matured, as discussed earlier.[172] Moreover, such legal weight is based in part upon the increasingly "quasi-judicial" nature and functioning of the Committee discussed above, as well as the formalization of the process of issuing General Comments. General Comments have heightened relevance also in an implementation context, which

---

[167] In Part IV of the Outline, the Committee also addresses the obligations of other relevant actors, other States Parties, Economic and Social Council, other United Nations Organizations, the relevant Specialized Agencies (Articles 2.1, 2.3, 18, 19, 20, 21, and 23 of the Covenant), and Civil Society.

[168] For example, legislation and domestic application of the ICESCR and other international instruments, State policies, institutions, legal remedies, reparation, and case law.

[169] Part VI of the Outline.

[170] Matthew Craven, *supra* n. 73, at 91.

[171] *See id.*

[172] *See* discussion of this issue in Part Two of this Study.

possesses no authoritative procedure for reconciling divergent interpretations of the ICESCR, and where States rarely comment on such interpretation.

The reporting system within which the General Comments operate has enhanced significance because of the absence of a process for individual communications or a system for interstate complaints.[173] The reporting system is thus a source of state practice, as much as the substantive steps States take to realize ICESCR rights, and in this way, can be taken as evidence of States Parties concurrence with the Committee's interpretations of ICESCR.[174] As Theodore Meron has observed, the "Committee may be competent to interpret the Covenant insofar as required for the performance of the Committee's functions. Such interpretation . . . affects their reporting obligations and their internal and external behaviour. It shapes the practice of States in applying the Covenant and may establish and reflect the agreement of the parties regarding its interpretation."[175]

Thus, States Parties' very involvement in the reporting process within which General Comments are embedded invests such Comments with a special authority and legitimacy, as does the fact that General Comments adopted are included in the Committee's annual report to ECOSOC, which is brought to the attention of the General Assembly.[176] Once again, States Parties' presence and involvement in the other organs of the United Nations for which the General Comments have relevance adds further to their "legal weight."

---

[173] The ICCPR has established such a system of interstate complaints. Article 41 provides "1. A State Party to the present Covenant may at any time declare under this article that it recognizes the competence of the Committee to receive and consider communications to the effect that a State Party claims that another State Party is not fulfilling its obligations under the present Covenant. Communications under this article may be received and considered only if submitted by a State Party which has made a declaration recognizing in regard to itself the competence of the Committee. No communication shall be received by the Committee if it concerns a State Party which has not made such a declaration . . ." The Article goes on to set detailed procedures for these communications. Article 41(2) states that the provisions of Article 41 would come into force when "ten States Parties to the present Covenant have made declarations under paragraph 1 of this article." Thus, Article 41 did not come into force and effect when the ICCPR entered into force on March 23, 1976, but rather on March 28, 1979, after the tenth State Party to the ICCPR had ratified it.

[174] *See* Matthew Craven, *supra* n. 73, at 91.

[175] Theodor Meron, *Human Rights Law-Making in the United Nations*, 10 (Oxford University Press 1986).

[176] The endorsement of the Committee's annual report containing the General Comment by the General Assembly is particularly significant given the resolution passed by the General Assembly, separately, on the same topic of the General Comment. In this case, Resolution 54/175 (*see supra* n. 32) and General Comment No. 15 (*see infra* n. 198) both address, *inter alia*, the issue of the human right to water.

Prior to General Comment No. 15 on the Right to Water, the Committee had issued a number of General Comments covering a wide range of issues, such as Reporting by States Parties;[177] International Technical Assistance Measures;[178] the Nature of States Parties Obligations;[179] the Right to Adequate Housing;[180] Persons with Disabilities;[181] Older Persons;[182] Adequate Housing and Forced Evictions;[183] the Relationship between Economic Sanctions and Respect for Economic, Social and Cultural Rights;[184] the domestic application of the Covenant;[185] Role of National Human Rights Institutions on the Protection of Economic, Social and Cultural Rights;[186] Plans of Action for Primary Education;[187] the Right to Adequate Food;[188] the Right to Education;[189] and the Right to the Highest Attainable Standard of Health.[190]

---

[177] General Comment No. 1, Reporting by States Parties (Third session, 1989), U.N. ECOSOC Supp. No 4, Annex III, at 87–9, U.N. Doc. E4-1989/22 (1989).

[178] General Comment No. 2, International Technical Assistance Measures (Art. 22 of the Covenant) (Fourth session, 1990), E/1990/23 Annex III.

[179] General Comment No. 3, The Nature of States Parties' Obligations (Art. 2, paragraph 1 of the Covenant) (Fifth session, 1990), E/1991/23 Annex III.

[180] General Comment No. 4, The right to adequate housing (Art. 11, paragraph 1 of the Covenant) (Sixth session, 1991), E/1992/23 Annex III.

[181] General Comment No. 5, Persons with disabilities (Eleventh session, 1994), U.N. Doc E/C.12/1994/13 (1994).

[182] General Comment No. 6, The economic, social and cultural rights of older persons (Thirteenth session, 1995), U.N. Doc. E/C.12/1995/16/Rev.1 (1995).

[183] General Comment No. 7, The right to adequate housing (Art. 11, paragraph 1 of the Covenant): forced evictions, U.N. Doc. E/C.12/1997/4 (1997). For a discussion of the right to adequate housing, as adopted under the South African Constitution, *see* the case of *Grootboom v. The Government of the Republic of South Africa* 2001 (1) SA 46, CC, *see infra* n. 294.

[184] General Comment No. 8, The relationship between economic sanctions and respect for economic, social and cultural rights (Seventeenth session, 1997), U.N. Doc. E/C.12/1997/8 (1997).

[185] General Comment No. 9, The domestic application of the Covenant (Nineteenth session, 1998), U.N. Doc. E/C.12/1998/24 (1998).

[186] General Comment No. 10, The role of national human rights institutions in the protection of economic, social and cultural rights (Nineteenth session, 1998), U.N. Doc. E/C.12/1998/24 (1998).

[187] General Comment No. 11, Plans of action for primary education (Art. 14) (Twentieth session, 1999), U.N. Doc. E/C.12/1999/4 (1999).

[188] General Comment No. 12, Right to adequate food (Art. 11) (Twentieth session, 1999), U.N. Doc. E/C.12/1999/5 (1999).

[189] General Comment No. 13, The right to education (Art. 13) (Twenty-first session, 1999), U.N. Doc. E/C.12/1999/10 (1999).

[190] General Comment No. 14, The right to the highest attainable standard of health (Twenty-second session, 2000), U.N. Doc. E/C.12/2000/4 (2000). It is worth noting in this regard that as early as 1946, the Constitution of the WHO stated in its Preamble, that the

General Comment No. 3 elaborated the States Parties' obligations under Article 2, paragraph 1, of the ICESCR.[191] It clarified that Article 2 must be seen as having a dynamic relationship with all the provisions of the ICESCR, and that the obligations arising therefrom are both obligations of conduct and result.[192] The Comment confirmed that the ICESCR "provides for progressive utilization and acknowledges the constraints due to the limits of available resources, it also imposes various obligations which are of immediate effect."[193] It noted two such obligations. The first relates to the undertaking by the States Parties to guarantee that the rights enunciated under the ICESCR ". . . will be exercised without discrimination of any kind of race, colour, sex, language, religion, political or any other opinion, national or social origin, property, birth or other status."[194] The second undertaking relates to the obligation "to take steps" to progressively achieve the full realization of the rights recognized under the ICESCR.[195] The Committee emphasized that such steps must be taken within a reasonably short period of time after the ICESCR's entry into force for the states concerned, and that such steps "should be deliberate, concrete and targeted as clearly as possible

---

enjoyment of the highest attainable standard of health is one of the fundamental rights of every human being. For the Constitution of the WHO *see* <http://policy.who.int/cgi-bin/om_isapi.dll?infobase=Basicdoc&softpage=Browse_Frame_Pg42>.

[191] *See supra* n. 179.

[192] *See id.*

[193] *See id.*, paragraph 1. Furthermore, paragraph 9 of the Comment states, "The concept of progressive realization constitutes a recognition of the fact that full realization of all economic, social and cultural rights will generally not be able to be achieved in a short period of time. In this sense the obligation differs significantly from that contained in article 2 of the International Covenant on Civil and Political Rights which embodies an immediate obligation to respect and ensure all of the relevant rights. Nevertheless, the fact that realization over time, or in other words progressively, is foreseen under the Covenant should not be misinterpreted as depriving the obligation of all meaningful content. It is on the one hand a necessary flexibility device, reflecting the realities of the real world and the difficulties involved for any country in ensuring full realization of economic, social and cultural rights. On the other hand, the phrase must be read in the light of the overall objective, indeed the raison d'être, of the Covenant which is to establish clear obligations for States parties in respect of the full realization of the rights in question."

[194] *See* Article 2 (2) of the ICESCR. In this regard, it is worth clarifying that Article 2 (3) of the ICESCR clarifies that "Developing countries, with due regard to human rights and their national economy, may determine to what extent they would guarantee the economic rights recognized under the present Covenant to non-nationals." Furthermore, Article 4 of the ICESCR states that ". . . the States may subject such rights only to such limitations as are determined by law only in so far as this may be compatible with the nature of these rights and solely for the purpose of promoting the general welfare in a democratic society."

[195] *See* Article 2 (1) of the ICESCR.

towards meeting the obligations recognized in the ICESCR."[196] It further noted that "any deliberately retrogressive measures in that regard would require the most careful consideration and would need to be fully justified by reference to the totality of the rights provided for in the Covenant and in the context of the full use of the maximum available resources."[197]

Thus, General Comments issued by the Committee on Economic, Social and Cultural Rights are reflective of the experience gained as a result of the examination of reports by the Committee on the various rights and issues covered under the ICESCR. While they do not, and indeed cannot, create "new obligations," they clearly elaborate upon and clarify existing obligations of the States Parties under the ICESCR. General Comments are therefore critical interpretations of the provisions of, and obligations under, the ICESCR, which have a significant bearing on the enforcement of the ICESCR, and the realization and observance of the rights it contains. This is all the more true in the context of an instrument (that is, the ICESCR) that provides for no treaty-based supervisory body. Because of that, the intergovernmental entity of ICESCR (that is, ECOSOC), saw fit to establish an independent supervisory body of experts to work within a system that provided for neither individual petitions, nor interstate complaints, thereby giving the Committee's General Comments a clear significance and obvious prominence.

General Comment No. 15—The Right to Water

General Comment No. 15 was issued by the Committee on Economic, Social and Cultural Rights at its Twenty-ninth session, held in Geneva, November 11 to 29, 2002.[198] The Comment underscores the fact that water is a limited natural

---

[196] Article 2 of the ICESCR specifies legislative measures as one of the steps to be taken. The Committee noted that, in addition to legislation, provision of judicial remedies for justiciable rights is another measure that could be considered appropriate. Furthermore, Paragraph 2 of General Comment No. 3 makes clear that the obligation under Article 2 (1) of the ICESCR "to take steps" is neither qualified nor limited by other considerations.

[197] *See supra* n. 179, paragraph 9. For further elaboration of the concept of the implementation of the ICESCR *see* the "Limburg Principles on the Implementation of the International Covenant on Economic, Social and Cultural Rights" Maastricht, June 2–6, 1986, at <http://www2.law.uu.nl/english/sim/instr/limburg.asp>. On the issue of violations of the ICESCR, *see* the "Maastricht Guidelines on Violations of Economic, Social and Cultural Rights," Maastricht, January 22–26, 1997, at <http://www2.law.uu.nl/english/sim/instr/maastricht.asp>.

[198] *See* Economic and Social Council, Committee on Economic, Social and Cultural Rights (Twenty-ninth session, Geneva, November 11–29, 2002), Substantive Issues Arising in the

resource and a public good fundamental for life and health.[199] It also emphasizes that water is a prerequisite for the realization of other human rights. The Comment is thorough and comprehensive.[200] The crux of General Comment No. 15 is Paragraph 2, which states:

> The human right to water entitles everyone to sufficient, safe, acceptable, physically accessible and affordable water for personal and domestic uses. An adequate amount of safe water is necessary to prevent death from dehydration, to reduce the risk of water-related diseases and to provide for consumption, cooking, personal and domestic hygienic requirements.

The Comment notes the fact that the adequacy of water required for the right of water may vary according to different conditions.[201] Yet, the Committee laid down three factors as applicable in all circumstances. The first of those factors is *availability*, which the Committee interpreted as meaning that the water supply for each person must be sufficient and continuous for personal and domestic uses.[202] The second factor is *quality,* which means that the water required for each

---

Implementation of the International Covenant on Economic, Social and Cultural Rights; General Comment No. 15 (2002), The right to water (arts. 11 and 12 of the International Covenant on Economic, Social and Cultural Rights, U.N. Doc. E/C.12/2002/11 (Twenty-ninth session, 2002). For the text of General Comment No. 15, *see* <http://sim.law.uu.nl/SIM/CaseLaw/ Gen_Com.nsf/0/40b3e2540d9d4cf041256cd00033594f?OpenDocument>. The Comment is also produced as appendix V to this Study.

[199] As discussed earlier, the United Nations General Assembly adopted a resolution on December 20, 2000, proclaiming the year 2003 as the "International Year of Freshwater." (*See* United Nations General Assembly Resolution A/Res/55/196 (2000)). *See also* <http:// www.un.org/events/water/> and *supra* n. 44. The Resolution encourages all Member States, the United Nations system, and all other actors to take advantage of the Year to increase awareness of the importance of freshwater and to promote action at the local, national, regional, and international levels. It further requests the Secretary-General to submit to the General Assembly at its fifty-seventh session a progress report on the preparations for the International Year of Freshwater. The General Comment was issued in November 2002, ostensibly to coincide with the International Year of Freshwater that was about to commence when the General Comment was issued. It should also be noted that the Comment was issued a few months before the Third World Water Forum held in Kyoto, Japan, in March 2003. *See supra* n. 28.

[200] General Comment No. 15 comprises 60 paragraphs divided into six parts: an introduction; normative content of the right to water; States Parties' obligations; violations; implementation at the national level; and obligations of actors other than states.

[201] *See* paragraph 12 of General Comment No. 15.

[202] *See* paragraph 12 (a) of General Comment No. 15. The Comment defines "continuous" as meaning that "the regularity of the water supply is sufficient for personal and domestic uses." *See* footnote 12 of the Comment. The Comment further indicates that the quantity of water available for each person should correspond to the WHO Guidelines. The WHO estimates the

personal or domestic use must be safe, and therefore free from microorganisms, chemical substances, and radiological hazards that constitute a threat to a person's health.[203] The third factor is *accessibility*, which, for the Committee, has four overlapping dimensions, namely, physical accessibility, economic accessibility, nondiscrimination, and information accessibility.[204]

The Comment calls on the States Parties to "adopt effective measures to realize, without discrimination, the right to water as set out in this General Comment."[205] The Committee did not satisfy itself with simply exhorting the States Parties to realize the right to water; it went further and based the right in a number of different ways that may be classified into three analytic devices: derivation and inference; centrality and necessity; and prior recognition. The Committee used those three elements to conclude that there is a human right to water, because this right is not

---

use by a household through a single tap within the confines of the household living area as typically about 50 liters per day, and considers this as access to an intermediate level of service, ensuring good hygiene. In case of supply of water through multiple taps within the house, the average use per person, per day is estimated as 100–200 liters. *See Right to Water (Health and Human Rights Publication Series, No. 3)* 13–14 (World Health Organization 2003). *See also,* Peter H. Gleick, *Basic Water Requirements for Human Activities: Meeting Basic Needs,* 21 Water International, 82 (1996).

[203] *See* paragraph 12 (b) of General Comment No. 15. Reference should be made, in this connection, to the large scale contamination of groundwater in Bangladesh with naturally occurring arsenic in the mid-1990s. That contamination resulted in more than 20 million people ingesting dangerous amounts of arsenic through groundwater. Bangladesh was compelled to seek world assistance for dealing with this serious water quality crisis. For a discussion of this situation, *see* Nadim Khouri & Sarwat Chowdhury, *Mitigating Natural Groundwater Contamination in Bangladesh: Early Policy Lessons From a Development Project* in *Groundwater—Legal and Policy Perspectives, Proceedings of a World Bank Seminar,* World Bank Technical Paper No. 456, 93 (Salman M. A. Salman, ed., 1999). The problem of unsafe drinking water is now taking different forms, and involves both developing and developed countries. *See* the European Court of Justice judgment against the United Kingdom and France on this issue of water quality; *see infra* n. 300. Addressing the elevated levels of lead in drinking water in Washington D.C., the United States Environmental Protection Agency stated in March 2004 that "According to the most recent information available, elevated levels of lead in District of Columbia drinking water are due to increased water corrosivity, and are aggravated in some homes by the presence of lead service lines." For more details on this issue *see* <http://www.epa.gov/dclead/> and *Against the Tide—Getting the Lead Out*, Time Magazine, April 5, 2004, at 59.

[204] *See* paragraph 12 (c) of General Comment No. 15. With regard to physical accessibility, the paragraph states that water and water facilities and services must be within safe physical reach of all sections of the population. Economic accessibility is defined in terms of affordability for all. Nondiscrimination means accessibility to all, including the most vulnerable and marginalized sections of the population, while information accessibility includes the right to seek, receive, and impart information concerning water issues.

[205] *See* paragraph 1 of General Comment No. 15.

explicitly provided for in the ICESCR, and because, by its nature, a General Comment does not alter the explicit provisions of the ICESCR, nor does it create new rights beyond the parameters of what is contained in the ICESCR.[206]

Derivation and Inference

The Committee relied in its Comment upon the derivation of a right to water from Article 11 of the ICESCR. The Article confirms recognition by the States Parties to the ICESCR of "the right of everyone to an adequate standard of living for himself and his family, including adequate food, clothing and housing, and to the continuous improvement of living conditions."[207] The Committee placed particular reliance on the provision on "including adequate food, clothing and housing." The process of implying rights is undertaken by relying on a well-established method of statutory interpretation in the realm of rights. The Committee set forth its methodology by stating that "The use of the word 'including' indicates that this catalogue of rights was not intended to be exhaustive."[208] "The right to water clearly falls within the category of guarantees essential for securing an adequate standard of living, particularly since water is one of the most fundamental conditions for survival."[209]

---

[206] As indicated earlier, there are no Protocols to the ICESCR. Proposals for a petition system under the ICESCR have been discussed on a number of occasions, but have not yet been finalized. *See supra,* n. 153.

[207] Article 11 (1) of the ICESCR states that "The States Parties to the present Covenant recognize the right of everyone to an adequate standard of living for himself and his family, including adequate food, clothing and housing, and to the continuous improvement of living conditions. The States Parties will take appropriate steps to ensure the realization of this right, recognizing to this effect the essential importance of international cooperation based on free consent."

[208] *See id.*

[209] This methodology is reminiscent of that employed by the Irish High Court in the case of *Ryan v. Attorney General* (1965) I.R. 294, which was the first case in which "unenumerated rights" were identified in the Irish Constitution (Bunreacht na hÉireann, 1937). Article 40.3 of the Constitution provides:

"40.3.1 The State guarantees in its laws to respect, and so far as is practicable, by its laws to defend and vindicate the personal rights of the citizen.

40.3.2 The State shall*, in particular*, by its laws protect as best it may from unjust attack, and in the case of injustice done, vindicate the life, person, good name, and property rights of every citizen" (emphasis added).

Unlike earlier courts, Judge Kenny did not treat these provisions as mere "umbrella" clauses that simply repeated protections provided elsewhere in the text and as adding nothing of substance. Rather, he treated Article 40.3.1. as separable from Article 40.3.2. That being so, he reasoned that the sweep of rights to which it refers goes beyond those specified in Article

The Committee went further and inferred this right also from Article 12 of the ICESCR where the States Parties recognized the right of everyone to the enjoyment of the highest attainable standard of physical and mental health,[210] concluding that the right to water is inextricably related to this right. It also tied the right to water to the other rights enshrined in the International Bill of Human Rights, "foremost amongst them the right to life and human dignity."[211]

It should be noted here that the early work of scholars on the subject of the human right to water followed, more or less, the approach of derivation and inference. Stephen McCaffrey, after noting that water was not mentioned at all in either of the 1966 United Nations Covenants on human rights, or the UDHR, concluded that "if there is a right to water under the basic instruments of international human rights law, therefore, it must be inferred."[212] Similarly, Peter Gleick, after discussing the provisions of each of the two Covenants, concluded that "As with the UDHR, access to water can be inferred as a derivative right accessory to meet the explicit rights to health and adequate standard of life."[213]

Another approach to the issue of the human right to water is linking it to environmental law. Although the Committee did not adopt this line of analysis, some authors have followed this approach.[214] The basis of this approach can be traced to the Stockholm Declaration, which stated that "man has the fundamental right to freedom, equality, and adequate conditions of life, in an environment of a quality that permits a life of dignity and well-being, and he bears a solemn responsibility to protect and improve the environment for present and future generations."[215] The underlying contention for deriving a human right to water

---

40.3.2 and indeed those specified elsewhere in the Constitution. The test provides for the identification of unspecified (but equally effective) rights whether they "fit" with the "democratic and Christian nature of the State," which is of course a curiously state-centered way of identifying human rights.

[210] Article 12 (1) of the ICESCR states that "The States Parties to the present Covenant recognize the right of everyone to the enjoyment of the highest attainable standards of physical and mental health."

[211] *See* paragraph 3 of General Comment No. 15. For a discussion of the International Bill of Rights *see supra* n. 12.

[212] Stephen McCaffrey, *supra* n. 79.

[213] Peter Gleick, *The Human Right to Water*, 1 Water Policy, 492 (1998).

[214] Luis Rodriguez-Rivera, *Is the Human Right to Environment Recognized Under International Law? It Depends on the Source*, 12 Colo. J. Int'l. Envtl. L. & Pol'y, 1 (2001).

[215] *See* Principle 1 of the Stockholm Declaration, *supra* n. 13.

from the emerging principles of environmental law is that there exists some form of individual human right to environment, as well as a general right of the environment, whereby states must acknowledge the importance of preserving nature for nature's sake.[216] The right to the environment can arguably serve as a basis for the right to water since each is clearly linked to the other. Under this approach, a state must uphold the right to water by providing for the basic needs of its people through a proper and adequate use of the state's natural resources.[217]

It should be added that a number of other experts in this field question the view that there is a right to a clean environment.[218] Perhaps because of the lack of a wider agreement to the notion of a right to a clean environment, the Committee on Economic, Social and Cultural Rights did not infer a right to water therefrom. It remains to be seen whether the Committee will one day issue a General Comment on the "Right to Clean and Healthy Environment," and whether that right, if and when it is issued, would be linked to, and further strengthen, the right to water.

---

[216] *See id.* In linking the right to environment to the rights enumerated under the ICESCR, Rodriguez-Rivera stated "Also, the right to environment can be defined as incorporating the substantive standards of recognized economic, social and cultural rights indispensable for the realization of human dignity, such as the right to a standard of living adequate for health and well being, the right to the highest attainable standard of mental and physical health, and the right to safe and healthy working conditions." *See supra* n. 214, at 11–12. In this regard, a reference to the Constitution of Brazil is apposite because of its inclusion of a specific provision on the right to the environment. Article 225 of the Constitution of Brazil states that "Everyone has the right to an ecologically balanced environment, which is a public good for the people's use and is essential for a healthy life. The Government and the community have a duty to defend and to preserve the environment for present and future generations." *See Constitution of the Federative Republic of Brazil* in *Constitutions of the Countries of the World*, Vol. III, 140, (Albert Blaustein & Gisbert Flanz, eds., Oceana Publications, Inc. 1971).

[217] For more discussion of this issue *see Water Resources and International Law*, Hague Academy of International Law, Centre for Studies and Research in International Law and International Relations, 101–104 (Report of the 2001 Session by Salman M. A. Salman and Laurence Boisson de Chazournes) (Martinus Nijhoff Publishers 2002). It is noted in that Report that "The problems with the environmentally oriented approach towards the human right to water is the inherent conflicts that have not been resolved when considering the needs of the person versus those of the environment, as well as the lack of normative clarity which leads towards an ambiguous and uncertain practical applicability of the human right to water." *See id.,* at 104.

[218] *See* Günther Handl, *Human Rights and Protection of the Environment: A Mildly 'Revisionist' View*, in *Human Rights, Sustainable Development and the Environment*, 117 (Antonio A. Cancado Trindade, ed., Instituto Interamericano de Derechos Humanos and Banco Interamericano de Desarrollo, 1995). *See also* Günther Handl, *Human Rights and Protection of the Environment*, in *Economic, Social and Cultural Rights: A Textbook*, 303 (Asbjørn Eide, Catarina Krause & Allan Rosas, eds., 2d ed., Martinus Nijhoff Publishers 2001).

Centrality and Necessity

Another model employed by the Committee was an analysis of the centrality of water to other ICESCR rights. The Comment notes the centrality of water to States Parties' duties under Article 1 (2) of the ICESCR. The Article states that a people shall not be "deprived of its means of subsistence"[219] and requires adequate access to water for subsistence farming. The right to the highest attainable standard of health (Article 12.1) provided yet another anchor,[220] because water is central to environmental hygiene. Similarly, the necessity of water to the right to adequate food, as well as to housing (Article 11.1), was also cited.[221]

Beyond the substantive content of the ICESCR provisions, the Committee reaffirmed the ineluctable place of water in the rights to life, liberty, and human dignity contained in the UDHR.[222] This analytic model offers significant reinforcement to the concept of a human right to water, because without water many of the rights contained in the core international human rights instruments would be meaningless and left devoid of any practical effect. The Committee noted this when it stated that "the right to water clearly falls within the category of guarantees essential for securing an adequate standard of living, particularly since it is one of the most fundamental conditions for survival."[223]

---

[219] Article 1 (2) of the ICESCR states that: "All peoples may, for their own ends, freely dispose of their natural wealth and resources without prejudice to any obligation arising out of international economic cooperation, based on the principle of mutual benefit, and international law. In no case may a people be deprived of its own means of subsistence." *See* paragraph 7 of General Comment No. 15.

[220] Article 12.1 of the ICESCR states that: "The States Parties to the present Covenant recognize the right of everyone to the enjoyment of the highest attainable standard of physical and mental health."

[221] Article 11.1 of the ICESCR states that: "The States Parties to the present Covenant recognize the right of everyone to an adequate standard of living for himself and his family, including adequate food, clothing and housing, and to the continuous improvement of living conditions. The States Parties will take appropriate steps to ensure the realization of this right, recognizing to this effect the essential importance of international co-operation based on free consent." For the right to adequate housing, *see also* General Comment No. 4, *supra* n. 180. The relationship between adequate housing and water lies in the fact that deprivation of any dwelling of water supply would render such dwelling unlivable. For the right to adequate food, *see* General Comment No. 12, *supra* n. 188. The centrality of water to at least three of the Millennium Development Goals (eradication of extreme poverty and hunger, reducing child mortality, and improving mental health) has already been discussed. *See supra* n. 42.

[222] Article 1 of the UDHR states in Article 1 that "All human beings are born free and equal in dignity and rights . . ." while Article 3 proclaims "Everyone has the right to life, liberty and security of person." *See supra* n. 59.

[223] *See* paragraph 3 of General Comment No. 15. Similarly, paragraph 6 of General Comment No. 15, emphasizing centrality of water, states that "Water is required for a range of different

Were the rights contained in the ICESCR interpreted in a highly literal fashion, or without taking account of the practical prerequisites of their realization, it would not be difficult to render the entire instrument ineffectual, and the commitments thereunder abstracted and hollow. Rights are not ideals suspended in an abstract context, but rather principles embodied in concrete undertakings that demand variable but substantive commitments on the part of the States Parties. Human rights are protected differently in different contexts and times, and their effective protection can in no way be viewed as static or unchanging, but rather as constantly evolving. This flux is further compounded by the fact that different human rights are deeply interwoven and are rarely realized in a singular or isolated manner, but rather exist in complex interdependency. Thus, the argument of the Comment that many human rights are interwoven around water, and cannot possibly be realized without a right to water, rests on a considerably solid basis.

Prior Recognition

The Committee also based a significant part of its argument on the right to water on the existence of other international legal instruments that recognize the right to water. In particular, the Committee cited Article 14 (2) of the International Convention on the Elimination of All Forms of Discrimination against Women (1979),[224] which provides that States Parties shall guarantee to women the right to "enjoy adequate living conditions, particularly in relation to housing, sanitation, electricity and water supply."[225] The Committee also cited Article 24 (2) of the Convention on the Rights of the Child, which stipulates that States Parties shall combat disease and malnutrition "through the provision of adequate nutritious foods and clean drinking water."[226] Other treaties that refer to the right to

---

purposes, besides personal and domestic uses, to realize many of the Covenant rights. For instance, water is necessary to produce food (right to adequate food) and ensure environmental hygiene (right to health). Water is essential for securing livelihoods (right to gain a living by work) and enjoying certain cultural practices (right to take part in cultural life)."

[224] Convention on the Elimination of All Forms of Discrimination against Women (generally referred to as CEDAW), entered into force on September 3, 1981, and as of March 2004, 176 States Parties out of the 177 signatories had ratified the instrument; U.N.T.S. No. 20378, vol. 1249 (1981). See <http://untreaty.un.org/ENGLISH/bible/englishinternetbible/partI/chapterIV/treaty10.asp>.

[225] *See id.*, Article 14.2 (h).

[226] Convention on the Rights of the Child, November 20, 1989, G.A. Res. 44/25, annex, 44 U.N. GAOR Supp. (No. 49) at 167, U.N. Doc. A/44/49 (1989); and 28 I.L.M 1448 (1989). The Convention has two optional protocols, one on the involvement of children in armed conflict, and

water include the Geneva Convention Relative to the Treatment of Prisoners of War (1949), Articles 20 and 26;[227] and the Geneva Convention Relative to the Treatment of Civilian Persons in time of War (1949), Articles 85, 89, and 127,[228] Articles 54 and 55 of Additional Protocol I thereto of 1977.[229] Articles 5 and 14

---

the other on the sale of children, child prostitution, and child pornography. Both protocols were adopted by the United Nations General Assembly on May 25, 2000 (General Assembly Resolution A/Res/54/263). The former entered into force on February 12, 2002, and the latter on January 18, 2002. *See* <http://www.unicef.org/crc/crc.htm>. As of March 2004, the Convention has been ratified by 192 countries (only the United States of America and Somalia are not parties to the Convention), *see* <http://untreaty.un.org/ENGLISH/bible/englishinternetbible/partI/chapterIV/treaty19.asp>.

[227] Geneva Convention relative to the Treatment of Prisoners of War, 75 U.N.T.S. 135, entered into force October 21, 1950. Article 20 of the Convention states:

> "The evacuation of prisoners of war shall always be effected humanely and in conditions similar to those for the forces of the Detaining Power in their changes of station.

> The Detaining Power shall supply prisoners of war who are being evacuated with sufficient food and potable water, and with the necessary clothing and medical attention. The Detaining Power shall take all suitable precautions to ensure their safety during evacuation, and shall establish as soon as possible a list of the prisoners of war who are evacuated . . . ;"

> Article 26 of the same Convention states ". . . Sufficient drinking water shall be supplied to prisoners of war."

[228] Geneva Convention relative to the Protection of Civilian Persons in Time of War. 75 U.N.T.S. 287, entered into force October 21, 1950. Article 85 provides, in relevant part:

> "Internees shall have for their use, day and night, sanitary conveniences which conform to the rules of hygiene and are constantly maintained in a state of cleanliness. They shall be provided with sufficient water and soap for their daily personal toilet and for washing their personal laundry; installations and facilities necessary for this purpose shall be granted to them.

> Showers or baths shall also be available. The necessary time shall be set aside for washing and for cleaning . . ."

Article 89 of the same Convention states:

> "Daily food rations for internees shall be sufficient in quantity, quality and variety to keep internees in a good state of health and prevent the development of nutritional deficiencies. Account shall also be taken of the customary diet of the internees.

> Internees shall also be given the means by which they can prepare for themselves any additional food in their possession.

> Sufficient drinking water shall be supplied to internees."

Article 127 of the same Convention states:

> ". . . The Detaining Power shall supply internees during transfer with drinking water and food sufficient in quantity, quality and variety to maintain them in good health, and also with the necessary clothing, adequate shelter and the necessary medical attention. The Detaining Power shall take all suitable precautions to ensure their safety during transfer, and shall establish before their departure a complete list of all internees transferred . . ."

[229] Protocol Additional to the Geneva Conventions of August 12, 1949, and relating to the Protection of Victims of International Armed Conflicts (Protocol 1), 1125 U.N.T.S. 3, entered into

of Additional Protocol II of 1977[230] were also referred to. The United Nations Convention on the Law of the Non-Navigational Uses of International Water-courses was also cited.[231] The Committee also referred to a number of declarations and resolutions, such as the Mar del Plata Action Plan of 1977;[232] the Dublin Statement of 1992;[233] Agenda 21 of the Rio Earth Summit, 1992

---

force December 7, 1978, in accordance with Article 95, 16 I.L.M 1391 (1977). Article 54—Protection of objects indispensable to the survival of the civilian population, states:

"1. Starvation of civilians as a method of warfare is prohibited.

2. It is prohibited to attack, destroy, remove or render useless objects indispensable to the survival of the civilian population, such as foodstuffs, agricultural areas for the production of foodstuffs, crops, livestock, drinking water installations and supplies and irrigation works, for the specific purpose of denying them for their sustenance value to the civilian population or to the adverse Party, whatever the motive, whether in order to starve out civilians, to cause them to move away, or for any other motive.

3. The prohibitions in paragraph 2 shall not apply to such of the objects covered by it as are used by an adverse Party:

(a) As sustenance solely for the members of its armed forces; or

(b) If not as sustenance, then in direct support of military action, provided, however, that in no event shall actions against these objects be taken which may be expected to leave the civilian population with such inadequate food or water as to cause its starvation or force its movement."

[230] Protocol Additional to the Geneva Conventions of August 12, 1949, and Relating to the Protection of Victims of Non-International Armed Conflicts (Protocol II), 1125 U.N.T.S. 609, entered into force December 7, 1978, 16 I.L.M 1442 (1977). Article 5—Persons whose liberty has been restricted, states:

"1. In addition to the provisions of Article 4, the following provisions shall be respected as a minimum with regard to persons deprived of their liberty for reasons related to the armed conflict, whether they are interned or detained:

(a) The wounded and the sick shall be treated in accordance with Article 7;

(b) The persons referred to in this paragraph shall, to the same extent as the local civilian population, be provided with food and drinking water and be afforded safeguards as regards health and hygiene and protection against the rigours of the climate and the dangers of the armed conflict;"

Article 14—Protection of works and installations containing dangerous forces, states:

"Starvation of civilians as a method of combat is prohibited. It is therefore prohibited to attack, destroy, remove or render useless, for that purpose, objects indispensable to the survival of the civilian population, such as foodstuffs, agricultural areas for the production of foodstuffs, crops, livestock, drinking water installations and supplies and irrigation works."

[231] The General Comment referred specifically to Article 10 (2) of the Convention, as well as the Statement of Understanding accompanying the Convention, drawing special attention to the requirement of providing sufficient water to sustain human life, when determining vital human needs. *See supra* n. 40.

[232] *See supra* n. 14.

[233] *See supra* n. 18. For a detailed discussion of those resolutions and declarations *see* Salman M. A. Salman, *supra* n. 34. It is noteworthy that the Committee missed mentioning the United

(UNCED);[234] as well as the Action Plan for the Johannesburg Summit on Sustainable Development, 2002.[235]

Precedents drawn from the Committee's own pronouncements were also reiterated. The Committee's previous recognition of the right to water in General Comment No. 6 (1995) on the economic, social, and cultural rights of older persons

---

Nations General Assembly Resolution on the Right to Development adopted on December 17, 1999, at the 83rd Plenary Meeting (Resolution 54/175), *supra* n. 32. As discussed earlier, the Resolution recalled the Declaration on the Right to Development (*supra* n. 75), and referred in the preamble to both the ICESCR and ICCPR. The Resolution further reaffirmed in paragraph 12 that, in the full realization of the right to development, *inter alia* "(a) the rights to food and clean water are fundamental human rights and their promotion constitutes a moral imperative both for national Governments and for the international community." The rest of the paragraph reaffirmed the right to shelter as a basic human right, and called on governments to take necessary action within their available resources to achieve the progressive realization of the right to health care services. The Resolution further urged all states to promote the right to development as a vital element in a balanced human rights program. This Resolution clearly strengthens the element of "prior recognition" on which the Committee based its argument for a human right to water. Similarly, Article 8 of the Declaration on the Right to Development can be read to strengthen the argument of prior recognition of the human right to water, because water is a basic resource and is a central element for food production. That Article reads "(1) States should undertake, at the national level, all necessary measures for the realization of the right to development and shall ensure, *inter alia*, equality of opportunity for all in their access to basic resources, education, health services, food, housing, employment and the fair distribution of income . . ." Another instrument that would strengthen the Committee's argument on the human right to water is the 1999 Protocol on Water and Health to the 1992 Convention on the Protection and Use of Transboundary Watercourses and International Lakes (United Nations Economic Commission for Europe—UN/ECE), 31 I.L.M. 1312 (1992). The Protocol on Water and Health was done in London, on June 17, 1999. The Protocol and many soft law documents ("recommendations" and "guidelines") related to the UN/ECE Water Convention are available on the Convention's homepage <http://www.unece.org/env/water/>. The objective of the Protocol, as stated in Article 1, is to promote the protection of human health and well-being through improving water management, including the protection of water ecosystems and through preventing, controlling, and reducing water-related diseases. Article 4 requires the Parties to the Protocol to take all appropriate measures for the purpose of ensuring (a) adequate supplies of wholesome drinking water which is free from any micro-organisms, parasites, and substances which, owing to their numbers or concentration, constitute a potential danger to human health . . . (b) adequate sanitation of a standard which sufficiently protects human health and the environment. Furthermore, Article 5 (l) requires that "Equitable access to water, adequate in terms both of quantity and of quality, should be provided for all members of the population, especially those who suffer a disadvantage or social exclusion." The integration of the right to adequate supplies of water and sanitation in Article 4 of the Protocol is a clear indication of the progressive nature of the Protocol. As discussed earlier, the Millennium Development Goals include the goal of reducing by half, by the year 2015, the proportion of people without sustainable access to safe drinking water. There was no mention of sanitation. This oversight was rectified two years later at the Johannesburg Summit on Sustainable Development when sanitation was added as a goal. *See supra* n. 43.

[234] *See supra* n. 21.

[235] *See supra* n. 43.

was reaffirmed.[236] Similarly, the Committee reiterated the fact that it had consistently addressed the right to water during its consideration of States Parties' reports, in accordance with its general guidelines regarding the form and content of reports to be submitted by States Parties under Articles 16 and 17 of the ICESCR, as well as in its other General Comments. The Committee also noted the importance of sustainable access to water resources for agriculture to realize the right to adequate food as elaborated in General Comment No. 12 (1999).[237]

Thus, General Comment No. 15 recognizes the human right to water through derivation and inferences from Articles 11 and 12 in the ICESCR, through an analysis of the centrality and necessity of water to other rights under the ICESCR and the other instruments under the Bill of Human Rights, as well as by basing its argument regarding the right to water on the existence of such a right under various other international legal instruments. Through these three analytical models, the Committee has provided a solid basis for recognizing a human right to water.

---

[236] *See supra* n. 182, at paragraph 5, which states "In 1991 the General Assembly adopted the United Nations Principles for Older Persons which, because of their programmatic nature, is also an important document in the present context. General Assembly resolution 46/91 of 16 December 1991, 'Implementation of the International Plan of Action on Ageing and related activities', annex. It is divided into five sections which correlate closely to the rights recognized in the Covenant. 'Independence' includes access to adequate food, water, shelter, clothing and health care." *See* also, paragraph 32, which states "Of the United Nations Principles for Older Persons, principle 1, which stands at the beginning of the section relating to the independence of older persons, provides that: 'Older persons should have access to adequate food, water, shelter, clothing and health care through the provision of income, family and community support and self-help'. The Committee attaches great importance to this principle, which demands for older persons the rights contained in article 11 of the Covenant."

[237] *See supra* n. 188.

PART FOUR
Legal and Policy Dimensions of General Comment No. 15

The human right to water implies considerable state responsibility and action. As General Comment No. 15 states, such a right would require action beyond the provision of water for drinking purposes, and would extend to water for environmental hygiene and health generally, as well as for growing food. It also involves accessibility, affordability, and nondiscriminatory access to water; protection against contamination by harmful substances and pathogenic microbes; and monitoring and combating aquatic ecosystems that serve as a habitat for disease.[238]

The Comment also classifies the nature and extent of the substantive obligations associated with the right to water in a number of ways. In particular, the Comment defines adequacy of water, as discussed earlier, in terms of availability, quality, and accessibility. The Comment elaborates upon the States Parties' obligations from a number of perspectives. In particular, the Comment emphasizes the need for progressive realization of the rights under the ICESCR, and, while recognizing the limits of available state resources, the Comment reiterates that various ICESCR obligations are of immediate effect.[239] As discussed earlier, such obligations include the guarantee that the right to water will be exercised without discrimination of any kind, and the obligation to take steps toward the full realization of the provisions of Articles 11 and 12 of the ICESCR. Such steps must be deliberate, concrete, and targeted toward the realization of the right to water.

As such, in line with the ICESCR, the General Comment defines the States Parties' obligations under the Comment as "constant and continuing"—meaning

---

[238] In this regard *see* the European Court of Justice judgment against the United Kingdom and France on this issue of water quality, *infra* n. 300; the case of arsenic contamination of groundwater in Bangladesh, *supra* n. 203; as well as the case of the elevated levels of lead in the District of Columbia drinking water, *supra* n. 203. The Committee on Economic, Social and Cultural Rights referred to estimates provided by the United Nations Commission on Sustainable Development that 2.3 billion people suffer each year from diseases linked to water; *see* United Nations Commission on Sustainable Development, *Comprehensive Assessment of Freshwater Resources of the World,* New York, 1997, p. 39, quoted in appendix V, n. 1, to this Study. Water-borne diseases are thought to have caused 3.4 million deaths in 1998, and it is reported that a child dies every 15 seconds from diarrhea caused largely by poor sanitation and water supply; *see supra* n. 42.

[239] General Comment No. 15, paragraph 17.

that the States Parties have a constant and continuing duty to move expeditiously and effectively toward the full realization of the right to water.[240]

Like many of the rights explicitly enshrined in the ICESCR, the right to water would require more than that the States Parties refrain from action, and would demand clear, positive action on their part, as well as the commitment of resources. As the Comment makes clear, the right to water involves not only freedoms, but also entitlements, more generally, that flow from the right and may entail obligations on the part of the State or even non-state actors.

The General Comment addresses this matter by stating explicitly that:

> The right to water contains both freedoms and entitlements. The freedoms include the right to maintain access to existing water supplies necessary for the right to water, and the right to be free from interference . . . By contrast, the entitlements include the right to a system of water supply and management that provides equality of opportunity for people to enjoy the right to water.[241]

In some respects, the right to water can more accurately be characterized as a need or an entitlement embodied as a right.[242] Thus, while some rights enhance the human condition and are critical for the development of a person's spiritual, emotional, moral, social, personal, and family existence, not all are indispensable to life itself. Similarly, while some rights ensure human flourishing, others, such as the right to water, are indispensable to bare physical subsistence.[243]

It should be noted that, while the full realization of the rights under the ICESCR is to be achieved progressively,[244] the General Comment establishes a strong presumption that retrogressive measures taken in relation to the right to water are prohibited under the Covenant.[245] The General Comment qualifies this prohibition by

---

[240] General Comment No. 15, paragraph 18.

[241] General Comment No. 15, paragraph 10.

[242] This classification can be inferred from the different resolutions, declarations, and action plans discussed in the first Part of this Study. As discussed in that Part, those instruments vacillated between dealing with water as a right or a need.

[243] There are a number of parallels that can be drawn between the normative analysis relevant to the right to water and the right to food. *See generally, The Right to Food* (Philip Alston & Katarina Tomaševski, eds., Martinus Nijhoff Publishers 1984).

[244] *See* Article 2(1) of the ICESCR, *supra* n. 93.

[245] Although paragraph 17 of General Comment No. 15 underscores the point about the progressive realization of the rights under the ICESCR, paragraph 18 of General Comment No. 15

stating that "If any deliberately retrogressive measures are taken, the State party has the burden of proving that they have been introduced after the most careful consideration of all alternatives and that they are duly justified by reference to the totality of the rights provided for under the Covenant in the context of the full use of the State party's maximum available resources."[246]

The General Comment elaborates a number of what it terms "specific legal obligations" that the Committee classified in three categories of obligations.[247] The Comment presents these obligations as "negative" duties of the States Parties, or duties that demand their forbearance. The first of these is the obligation to *respect,* which is essentially an obligation requiring that States Parties refrain from interference directly or indirectly with the enjoyment of the right to water. This requires that States Parties refrain from engaging in any practice that denies or limits equal access to adequate water, or arbitrarily interferes with customary or traditional arrangements for water allocation, or unlawfully diminishes or pollutes water. It also requires the States Parties to refrain from any action that limits access to or destroys water services or infrastructure as punitive measures. The obligations are essentially "negative" in nature, and resemble those traditionally associated with civil and political rights.[248]

A second type of obligation enunciated in the Comment involves the obligation to *protect,* which requires the States Parties to prevent third parties from interfering in any way with the enjoyment of the right to water.[249] This obligation

---

could be read as overstating the capabilities of the States Parties. That paragraph reads in part "Realization of the right should be feasible and practicable, since all States Parties exercise control over a broad range of resources, including water, technology, financial resources and international assistance, as with all other rights in the Covenant." The Committee itself has raised the possibility of resource constraints when it stated in paragraph 41 of General Comment No. 15, that "if resource constraints render it impossible for a State Party to comply fully with Covenant obligations, it has the burden of justifying that every effort has nevertheless been made to use all available resources . . ." It should also be noted that the Committee had acknowledged in General Comment No. 3, "the constraints due to the limits of available resources . . ." of the States Parties to the ICESCR, *see supra* n. 179.

[246] *See* paragraph 19 of General Comment No. 15. *See also* paragraph 9 of General Comment No. 3, *supra* n. 179, and *supra* n. 197.

[247] *See* paragraphs 20–29 of General Comment No. 15.

[248] For an insightful discussion of the nature and scope of States Parties' obligations under the ICESCR and, in particular, of the distinctions drawn between these obligations and those traditionally associated with the ICCPR, including the positive/negative rights dichotomy, *see* Philip Alston & Gerard Quinn, *supra* n. 73.

[249] *See* paragraphs 23–24 of General Comment No. 15.

includes, *inter alia*, adopting the necessary and effective legislative and other measures to restrain third parties from denying equal access to adequate water. Protection also requires preventing third parties, when they control or operate water services, from compromising equal, affordable, and physical access to sufficient, safe, and acceptable water.

A third type of obligation pronounced by the Comment is the obligation to *fulfill*, which the Comment explains can be disaggregated into obligations to facilitate, promote, and provide.[250] The obligation to facilitate requires that States Parties take positive measures to assist individuals and communities to enjoy the right to water. The obligation to promote obliges the States Parties to take steps to ensure that there is appropriate education concerning the hygienic use of water, protection of water sources, and methods to minimize water wastage. The obligation to provide refers to the need for States Parties to adopt the necessary measures directed toward the full realization of the right to water, such as granting sufficient recognition to the right within national, political, and legal systems; adopting a national water strategy; and ensuring that water is affordable for everyone.[251]

Having clarified the specific legal obligations with regard to the right to water, the General Comment goes further and identifies the circumstances where there may be violations to the right to water. Indeed, the Comment sets in motion a process that facilitates identification of violations, based on application of the normative content of the right to water to the obligations of the States Parties to the

---

[250] *See* paragraphs 25–29 of General Comment No. 15.

[251] In addition to those "Specific Legal Obligations" discussed above, the Comment elaborates on what it termed "Core Obligations." The Committee traced the concept of Core Obligations to General Comment No. 3, where "the Committee confirms that States Parties have a core obligation to ensure the satisfaction of, at the very least, minimum essential levels of each of the rights enunciated in the Covenant." The Committee identified a number of core obligations in relation to the right to water. Paragraph 37 sets forth nine such obligations, which can be summarized as follows: (a) ensuring access to the minimum amount of water that is safe and sufficient; (b) ensuring the right of access to water and water facilities on a nondiscriminatory basis; (c) ensuring physical access to water facilities or services that provide sufficient, safe, and regular water; (d) ensuring that personal safety is not threatened when having to physically access water; (e) ensuring equitable distribution of all available water facilities and services; (f) adopting and implementing a national water strategy and plan of action addressing the whole population, on the basis of participatory and transparent processes; (g) monitoring the extent of the realization or the nonrealization of the right to water; (h) adopting relatively low-cost targeted water programs to protect vulnerable and marginalized groups; and (i) taking measures to prevent, treat, and control diseases linked to water.

ICESCR. Applying the general principles of international law, the Comment starts with the premise that failure to act in good faith to take the necessary and feasible steps toward the realization of the right to water amounts to a violation of this right. However, keeping in mind the provisions of Article 2 of the ICESCR, the General Comment distinguishes between the inability and the unwillingness of a State Party to comply with its obligations in relation to the right to water. A State Party that is unwilling to use the maximum of its available resources for the realization of the right to water is in violation of its obligations under the ICESCR. However, if resource constraints render it impossible for a State Party to comply fully with its obligations under the ICESCR, the State has the burden of justifying that every effort has nevertheless been made to use all available resources to meet the obligations under the ICESCR. [252]

The General Comment makes clear that violations to the right to water can occur through either "acts of commission" or "acts of omission."[253] Acts of commission include the adoption of retrogressive measures incompatible with the States Parties' core obligations,[254] the formal repeal or suspension of legislation related to the right to water, or the adoption of legislation or policies that are incompatible with preexisting domestic or international legal obligations in relation to the right to water. Omissions, on the other hand, include the failure to take appropriate steps toward the full realization of everybody's right to water, the failure to have a national policy on water, or the failure to enforce the relevant laws. The Committee used the specific legal obligations that it has developed in relation to the right to water (the obligations to respect, to protect, and to fulfill) to identify examples of violations of such a right.

Violations of the obligation to respect follow from the State Party's interference with the right to water, and include arbitrary or unjustified disconnections, discriminatory or unaffordable increases in water tariffs, or pollution and diminution of water resources affecting human health. Violations of the obligation to protect follow from the failure of a State Party to take all necessary measures to safeguard persons within its jurisdiction from infringement of the right to water by a third party. Such violations include failure to enact or enforce laws

---

[252] *See* paragraph 41 of General Comment No. 15.

[253] *See* paragraphs 42 and 43 of General Comment No. 15.

[254] *See supra* n. 251 for the "Core Obligations" under the General Comment.

to prevent the contamination and inequitable extraction of water, failure to effectively regulate and control water services providers, or failure to protect water distribution systems. Violations of the obligations to fulfill occur through the failure of States Parties to take the necessary steps to ensure the realization of the right to water. Such violations include failure to adopt or implement a national water policy designed to ensure the right to water, failure to take measures to reduce the inequitable distribution of water facilities and services, and failure to take into account the state's international obligations.[255]

The General Comment highlights repeatedly the issue of affordability of water, in relation to both the specific legal obligations and the violations of such obligations. But does affordability mean that water should or can be given free of charge? This is an area in which the Comment is problematic, in that it appears to equate low cost water with free water. It specifically states that "to ensure that water is affordable, States Parties must adopt the necessary measures that may include, *inter alia,* (a) use of a range of appropriate low-cost techniques and technologies, (b) appropriate policies such as free or low cost water, and (c) income supplements."[256]

Most, if not all, water resources specialists would argue strongly against free water. Demand management would by necessity require some form of pricing of water.[257] Free water is an invitation for misuse and abuse. As the Dublin Principles state, "Past failure to recognize the economic value of water has led to waste-

---

[255] *See* paragraph 44 of General Comment No. 15.

[256] *See* paragraph 27 of General Comment No. 15. The paragraph further explains the concept of affordability by stating that "Any payment for water services has to be based on the principle of equity, ensuring that these services, whether privately or publicly provided, are affordable for all, including socially disadvantaged groups. Equity demands that poorer households should not be disproportionately burdened with water expenses as compared to richer households." One interpretation of the General Comment states that households can no longer be disconnected from water supplies, and that cost recovery principles would only be applied beyond meeting basic needs. *See International Rivers and Lakes*, a newsletter prepared jointly by the Department for Economic and Social Affairs, United Nations, New York, and the Economic Commission for Latin America and the Caribbean, Santiago, Chile, No. 38, December 2002, at 2 and 3. This interpretation goes beyond paragraph 10 of the Comment, which only addresses freedom "from arbitrary disconnections."

[257] Some cultures view water as a God-given gift for which no price should be charged. *See* Dante Caponera, *Water Laws in Moslem Countries*, FAO Irrigation and Drainage Papers No. 20, Vol 1, 11 (Food and Agriculture Organization of the United Nations 1973). *See also* Dante Caponera, *National and International Water Law and Administration, Selected Writings*, 73 (Kluwer Law International 2003). One possible way for addressing such cultural notions about water has been to argue that the price paid is for recovery of the cost of the service delivery of water, and not necessarily for the water itself.

ful and environmentally damaging uses of the resource. Managing water as an economic good is an important way of achieving efficient and equitable use, and of encouraging conservation and protection of water resources."[258] The World Commission for Water in the 21st Century went even further in addressing this issue when it stated, "Full-cost pricing of water services with equity will be needed to promote conservation and attract the very large investments that are needed. Polluter pays and user pays principles must be enforced. And mechanisms must be found whereby those who use water inefficiently have incentives to desist and transfer that water to higher-value uses, including environmental purposes."[259]

Indeed, the General Comment itself urges the States Parties to adopt comprehensive measures and programs to ensure that there is sufficient and safe water for present and future generations.[260] To achieve such sustainable use of water resources, the General Comment suggests nine methods, which include reducing depletion of water resources through unsustainable extraction, and increasing the efficient use of water by end users.[261] Operationalization of both methods would by necessity require pricing of water.

Despite the calls for cost recovery and full water pricing, innovative approaches have been developed to address the issue of affordability by the poor segment of the society. In Durban, South Africa, for example, the law provides that everybody is entitled to six free kiloliters of water per month, and is required to pay for any water consumption beyond that figure.[262] In Chile, a water stamps

---

[258] For the Dublin Principles *see supra* n. 18.

[259] World Commission for Water in the 21st Century, World Water Vision, Commission Report, *A Water Secure World: Vision for Water, Life and the Environment*, 3 (2000). Indeed, growing unavailability and increased competition for water resources require, as the World Water Assessment Programme stated, that water demands be well managed, so that water is efficiently used. The World Water Assessment Programme pointed out that some form of demand management must ultimately be applied, and that the use of pricing is an effective instrument in this regard. *See supra* n.1, at 337.

[260] *See* paragraph 28 of General Comment No. 15.

[261] The other methods listed in paragraph 28 include the following: reducing and eliminating contamination of watersheds; monitoring water reserves; ensuring that proposed developments do not interfere with access to adequate water; assessing the impacts of actions that may impinge upon water availability; reducing water wastage in its distribution; response mechanisms for emergency situations; and establishing competent institutions and appropriate institutional arrangements to carry out strategies and programs.

[262] *See Manquele v. Durban Transitional Metropolitan*, Council Case No. 2036/2000, at <http://www.communitylawcentre.org.za/localgov/bulletin2001/2001_1_manquele.php# manquele>. For a detailed discussion of this case, *see infra*, n. 298.

system for families who are below the poverty line was introduced, and such vouchers can be used to pay their water bills.[263] In Armenia, the law provides for financial assistance in the form of subsidies to needy users, or tax benefits to suppliers.[264]

The concept of affordability leads to another related issue, and that is the private sector participation in water resources management. While proponents of participation of the private sector argue that only the private sector can bring the desperately needed resources to the water sector,[265] legitimate questions have been raised about the inevitable increases in tariffs that poor people cannot afford, and that, in turn, would threaten the concept of the human right to water. This is not a theoretical situation. The case of the city of Cochabamba in Bolivia provides a vivid example to this effect.[266] Privatization of the water services there resulted in a considerable increase in the cost of water to the users whereby "some bills had doubled, and ordinary workers now had water bills that amounted to a quarter of their monthly income."[267] That resulted in widespread civil unrest, and consequently, the Bolivian government decided to cancel the contract with the private sector operator. Similar situations have arisen in other parts of Latin

---

[263] In Santiago, Chile, the government realized the contradiction in requiring the water utility to function as a commercial entity and at the same time provide subsidized water to the poor. "Accordingly, the government decided to institute a targeted, means-tested, government-administered 'water stamps' program, whereby poor people get 'stamps' to cover part of their water bill. The utility then not only strengthened its focus . . . but now had a clear incentive to serve the poor, who became revenue-generating customers like all others. The system works well." *See* World Water Council, World Water Vision, (Commission Report), *A Water Secure World: Vision for Water, Life, and the Environment,* 36 (2000).

[264] The Water Code of the Republic of Armenia (adopted on June 4, 2002) provides in Article 81 that the state may provide financial assistance in the form of subsidies or tax benefits to water suppliers as well as water users to ensure equal conditions and to avoid discrimination in the supply of water. One of the considerations for receiving such assistance is the financial situation of the person applying. Implementation of this Article of the Water Code requires the issuance of further procedures by the government for putting the subsidies and tax benefits into effect.

[265] The Report of the World Panel on Financing Water Infrastructure, *Financing Water for All* (World Water Council 2003) estimates the cost of meeting the Millennium Development Goal of reducing by half the proportion of people without sustainable access to adequate quantities of affordable safe water and sanitation as US$180 billion annually, up from the current figure of US$75 billion. *See id.,* at 3.

[266] For a full account of the story of privatization of water services in Cochabamba and its aftermath, *see* William Finnegan, *Letter from Bolivia—Leasing the Rain,* The New Yorker, April 8, 2002, at 43. It is worth noting that the organizers of the civil disobedience in Cochabamba vowed "to treat water as a human right." *See id.,* at 53.

[267] *See id.,* at 47.

America and Asia, as well as in South Africa.[268] The Cochabamba case is now pending before the International Centre for Settlement of Investment Disputes (ICSID)[269] of the World Bank Group.[270] Another problem associated with private sector participation in water services, similar to what occurred Cochabamba, is that the increase in tariffs usually takes place before any improvements in service delivery, which has meant that the consumers "were simply paying more for the same poor service."[271]

In this connection, General Comment No. 15, referring to the private sector as third parties, calls on the States Parties to prevent such third parties (when they operate or control water services) from compromising equal, affordable, and physical access to sufficient, safe, and acceptable water.[272] Prevention of such abuses, according to the General Comment, requires establishing an effective

---

[268] Finnegan claims that water privatizations have backfired across Latin America. By way of examples, he indicates that such privatization has cost the president of Panama his bid for reelection, forced the government of Argentina to cancel a number of contracts with one private sector operator, and that "Protests against water privatization have also erupted in Indonesia, Pakistan, India, South Africa, Poland and Hungry." *See id.,* at 53.

[269] *See Aguas del Tunari S.A. v. Republic of Bolivia* (Case No. ARB/02/3). The case was registered by ICSID on February 25, 2002, and a Tribunal for considering the case was constituted on July 5, 2002. For more on the status of the case, and on ICSID, *see* <http://www.icsid.org/>. *See also* ICSID Annual Report 2003, particularly Annex 2, "Disputes Before the Centre." There are two other cases pending before ICSID that relate to water: *Compania de Aguas del Aconquija S.A. and Vivendi Universal (formerly Compagnie General Des Eaux) v. Argentine Republic* (Case No. ARB/97/3) 41 I.L.M 1135 (2002); and *Azurix Corp. v. Argentine Republic* (Case No. ARB/01/12). The fact that three cases relating to the role of the private sector in water services are now pending before ICSID has been widely used by those opposed to private sector participation in water services as evidence of the failure of this experiment.

[270] The World Bank Group consists of five organizations, each of which is a separate legal and financial entity. Those organizations are the International Bank for Reconstruction and Development (IBRD), the International Development Association (IDA), the International Finance Corporation (IFC), the Multilateral Investment Guarantee Agency (MIGA), and the International Centre for Settlement of Investment Disputes (ICSID). For a general discussion of the structure and functions of those organizations *see* The World Bank, *A Guide to the World Bank,* 10–23 (The World Bank 2003); and The World Bank Annual Report, 2003, Volume 1, at 8–9.

[271] *See Bolivia Water Management: A Tale of Three Cities,* World Bank Operations Evaluation Department, Précis Number 222, 3 (Spring 2002).

[272] *See* paragraph 24 of General Comment No. 15. For a detailed discussion of the problems raised by private sector participation in the water and sanitation sector, and the case of the Cochabamba in particular, *see* Economic and Social Council, Commission on Human Rights, Economic, Social and Cultural Rights—Human Rights, Trade and Investment—Report of the High Commissioner for Human Rights (E/CN.4/Sub.2/2003/9, July 3, 2003). The Report underscored the concerns regarding private sector participation in the water sector. It states that "While promoting investment through private sector participation in the water and sanitation sector might be a possible strategy to upgrade the sector, there is concern that private

regulatory system, which would include independent monitoring, genuine public participation, and imposition of penalties for noncompliance.[273]

Another issue raised by the right to water in general and the General Comment in particular is that of the management of water resources, and the role of users in such management. The General Comment, limiting itself strictly to the role of interpretation and elaboration of the rights enshrined under the ICESCR, is silent on the issue of participation of the users in the operation and management of water resources. It could be argued that the notion of the human right to water connotes a passive approach to water resources management because it does not place any corresponding duties on those who are to be conferred with this right. In other words, the notion is unclear with regard to overall water resources management.[274] In this connection, General Comment No. 15 is silent on the issue regarding the duties or obligations of those upon whom the human right to water is conferred. There is no mention in the Comment of any duties for the users, such as the duty to conserve water, use it in a sustainable manner, or protect and pay for it.[275] Part III of the Comment deals with States Parties Obligations,[276] and Part VI deals with Obligations of Actors Other than States. There is no mention in either part of the obligations of the users. Similarly, the Core Obligations under the General Comment[277] relate exclusively to those of the States Parties, and do not include any reference to those of individuals. The issues surrounding the use and protection of water resources are complex, and responsibilities for such issues cannot be placed solely on the states. Individuals should bear an equal, if not a larger, portion of such responsibilities. The failure of the General Comment

---

sector participation might threaten the goal of basic service provision for all, particularly the poor, and transform water from being an essential life source to primarily an economic good." *See id.,* at 26. It is estimated that some 80 percent of those who have no access to improved sources of drinking water are the rural poor. It is quite unlikely that the private sector would see sufficient financial incentives to work in those rural areas.

[273] *See* paragraph 24 of General Comment No. 15. Furthermore, paragraph 33 obliges the States Parties to take steps to prevent their own citizens and companies from violating the right to water in other countries (i.e., host countries to the investment).

[274] *See* Jan Lundqvist, *Rules and Roles in Water Policy and Management—Need for Clarification of Rights and Obligations,* 25 Water International, 194 (2000).

[275] Although neither of the two Covenants include references to duties of individuals, it should be recalled that the UDHR deals in Article 29 with such duties; *see supra* n. 59 and n. 63.

[276] This is the longest part of the General Comment and includes more than 20 separate paragraphs.

[277] *See* paragraph 37 of the General Comment, discussed *supra* n. 251.

to address this issue is unfortunate and can arguably be considered a shortcoming of the Comment.

Along those lines it is also argued that, rather than placing emphasis on the recognition of a human right to water, a more pragmatic approach would be to address the right to manage, or participate in the management of, the water resources. As suggested by Jan Lundqvist "the critical point to ensure that fundamental human rights to water and sanitation are met will therefore be to ensure that actors other than the government will be allowed and supported to engage themselves in water management."[278] This approach was emphasized in 1992 by the Dublin Statement on Water and Sustainable Development.[279] The second of the Dublin Principles emphasizes that water development and management should be based on a participatory approach involving users, planners, and policymakers.[280] This participatory approach further strengthens the empowerment of the users, vesting them with both rights and corresponding duties with respect to water.[281] Needless to say, in order for participation to be meaningful and effective, a reasonable measure of free expression and assembly must be permitted. This interrelationship between participation and the need for a space for free expression and assembly is a clear indicator of the interdependence of social and economic rights on the one hand, and political and civil rights on the other.[282]

Indeed, the participation of users in the management of the water facilities has been viewed as an alternative to privatization of such water services or facilities. The case of the Santa Cruz water utility in Bolivia provides a vivid example of this. The utility is a consumer cooperative, governed by a general delegate assembly that appoints senior management. The utility has been part of Santa Cruz city

---

[278] *See supra* n. 274.

[279] *See supra* n. 18.

[280] For the Dublin Principles *see supra* n. 18. Similarly, Article 5 (f) of the Protocol on Water and Health (*supra* n. 233) requires in Article 5 (f) that "Action to manage water resources should be taken at the lowest appropriate administrative level."

[281] The World Bank Water Resources Management Policy Paper (1993) stresses this notion of users' participation. The Paper states, "The participation of users in managing and maintaining water facilities and operations brings many benefits. Participation in planning, operating, and maintaining irrigation works and facilities to supply water and sanitation services increases the likelihood that these will be well maintained and contributes to community cohesion and empowerment in ways that can be spread to other development activities." *See id.,* at 55. *See also* Salman M. A. Salman, *The Legal Framework for Water Users' Associations, A Comparative Study*, World Bank Technical Paper No. 360, 2 (1997).

[282] *See supra* n. 81 and n. 82.

for more than 20 years, "and continues to enjoy the reputation as one of the best utilities in Latin America,"[283] so much so that the Operations Evaluation Department of the World Bank indicated that "The Bolivia experience demonstrates that cooperative solutions can be superior to either public or private approaches to utility management."[284] This example illustrates how users' participation in water management could be used as an effective tool for administration and financing of water facilities, which in turn would assist in the realization of the right to water.

It is worth adding in this regard that the General Comment addresses the issue of people's participation in connection with the formulation and implementation of national water strategies and plans of action, but not in connection with actual operation and management of water resources.[285] This is regrettable, because both issues have a strong bearing on the practical ramifications of the human right to water.

International obligations of the States Parties to the ICESCR occupy an important place in the Comment, and are dealt with in paragraphs 30 to 36 thereof. The Comment exhorts States Parties to comply with international obligations in relation to the right to water, asserting that international cooperation requires States Parties to refrain from actions that interfere, directly or indirectly, with the enjoyment of the right to water in other countries.[286] It also calls

---

[283] For a discussion of the reasons behind the success of the Santa Cruz water utility, *see* World Bank Operations Evaluation Department, Précis Number 222, *supra* n. 271 at 2. The Précis noted the transparent and efficient administration that has virtually eliminated corruption, and earned the utility two World Bank loans that were used "to great advantage through efficient implementation and operation." *See id.,* at 2.

[284] *See id.,* at 3. In addition to Santa Cruz, the Précis discussed the cases of La Paz/El Alto and Cochabamba. With regard to La Paz/El Alto, although the Précis noted the success of the privatization experience, it indicated that "higher tariffs have reduced per capita consumption from 110 to 87 litres per person per day—undercutting income such that the concessionaire is considering a campaign to promote water use." This is quite ironic, and indeed very unfortunate, given that the whole idea behind pricing water is to manage demand, and promote efficient use and conservation. For further discussion of the issue *see* William Finnegan, *supra* n. 266, at 53.

[285] *See* paragraph 48 of General Comment No. 15. That paragraph further states that "The right of individuals and groups to participate in decision-making processes that may affect their exercise of the right to water must be an integral part of any policy, programme or strategy concerning water. Individuals and groups should be given full and equal access to information concerning water, water services and the environment, held by public authorities or third parties."

[286] The Comment notes that the United Nations Convention on the Law of the Non-Navigational Uses of International Watercourses requires that human needs be taken into account in determining the equitable and reasonable utilization of watercourses. *See supra* n. 198, at Article 31.

on the States Parties to refrain from imposing embargoes or similar measures that prevent the supply of water, as well as the goods and services essential for securing the right to water.[287]

The issue of international obligations has been dealt with extensively by McCaffrey, who asked, "is there a right under international law to receive water from a co-riparian country?"[288] After a thorough analysis of the question, he opined that Article 10 of the U.N. Watercourses Convention gives priority to the use of water for drinking purposes in one state, over its use for hydropower generation, or agriculture in another riparian state.[289] Elaborating on this point, McCaffrey concluded, "On the international level, it seems equally clear that one state cannot deny a co-riparian state water necessary for the survival of the latter's population on the ground that the water is needed for the economic development of the former."[290] Although the Convention has not yet entered into force, many of its principles, such as the principle of equitable and reasonable utilization, and the obligation not to cause significant harm, reflect customary international law.[291] Thus, while the Comment does not seem to have contributed much to the issue of the obligations of the riparians to each other under the principles of international water law, it nevertheless has the value-added of highlighting the issue as part of the overall concept of the human right to water.

As a part of the section on "International obligations," the Comment calls on all international organizations and institutions to cooperate effectively with States in relation to the right to water at the domestic level, and to take into account the right to water in their actions and policies.[292]

---

[287] The Committee referred here to General Comment No. 8 on the relationship between economic sanctions and respect for economic, social, and cultural rights. *See supra* n. 184.

[288] *See* Stephen McCaffrey, *supra* n. 79, at 17. For discussion of Article 10 of the U.N. Watercourses Convention, *see supra* n. 35 and accompanying text.

[289] *See* Stephen McCaffrey, *supra* n. 79, at 22.

[290] *See id.*, at 24.

[291] *See* Stephen McCaffrey, *The UN Convention on the Law of the Non-Navigational Uses of International Watercourses: Prospects and Pitfalls*, in Salman M. A. Salman and Laurence Boisson de Chazournes, eds., *supra* n. 35, at 26–27.

[292] It is worth noting that in addition to mentioning the United Nations agencies, the Comment urged that the international financial institutions, "notably the International Monetary Fund and the World Bank, should take into account the right to water in their lending policies, credit agreements, structural adjustment programs and other development projects . . . so that the enjoyment of the right to water is promoted." *See* paragraph 60 of General Comment No. 15. Paragraph 36 of General Comment No. 15 urged "the States Parties that are

Thus, it is submitted that the General Comment on the right to water does not create *new* obligations for States Parties. Rather, the Comment gives definition to certain of the ICESCR's explicit provisions, and extrapolates the obligations these entail. In this, it merely elaborates upon rights and obligations acceded to by States Parties, rights that the States Parties have already undertaken to realize. It makes explicit the existence of a right to water as it inheres in the ICESCR, both in those rights specifically provided for in that instrument, and as a result of the context in which the ICESCR is currently interpreted and implemented.

This conclusion is also rooted in the manner in which the Committee approached the definition of the right to water: it is a right identified by derivation, centrality, and necessity. In this way, it inheres already in the ICESCR. The methodology employed by the Committee guards, at least in part, against accusations of activism and an excess of creativity. The Committee has also grounded the right to water in rights already explicitly provided for under other legal international instruments. The right to water is therefore a human right because it is a part of other human rights, and is indispensable to the realization of those rights, as well as to the right to life itself. Its recognition, therefore, hinges on the fact that it is a precondition for the realization of the numerous other human rights. This is because there are a number of rights contained in the ICESCR that would be difficult to realize without water, and this would strengthen the basis for the concept of human right to water. As such, the General Comment follows the approach that these rights require a right to water in order to be realized, and are, as such, not otherwise realizable.

---

members of international financial institutions, notably the International Monetary Fund, the World Bank and the regional development banks, should take steps to ensure that the right to water is taken into account in their lending policies, credit agreements and other international measures." Although paragraph 36 of the Comment mentions the International Monetary Fund and the World Bank indirectly (through the States Parties that are members of those organizations), paragraph 60 makes a direct reference to the International Monetary Fund and the World Bank. The reference to the World Bank in General Comment No. 15 is interesting given the Agreement between the United Nations and the International Bank for Reconstruction and Development (the World Bank), which entered into force on November 15, 1947. Article I (2) of the Agreement states that the Bank is a specialized agency, but "by reason of the nature of its international responsibilities and the terms of its Articles of Agreement, the Bank is, and is required to function as, an independent international organization." Moreover, Article IV (2) of the same Agreement states that "neither organization, nor any of their subsidiary bodies, will present any formal recommendations to the other without reasonable prior consultation with regard thereto." For the provisions of the Agreement, *see* 16 U.N.T.S. 346 (1948).

Although it is too early to measure the impact the General Comment has had thus far on the issue of the human right to water, the fact remains that this Comment is having far-reaching effects, relative to the other General Comments issued by the Committee. This may be attributable to the fact that the debate on the human right to water has been at the top of the agenda in a number of international forums, including the General Assembly of the United Nations. Moreover, the importance of this particular General Comment has been underscored by the procedural mechanisms employed by the Committee to recognize such a right. This recognition has been achieved through derivation of such a right from, and its centrality to, other rights under the ICESCR, as well as prior recognition of such a right in some other international conventions, agreements, resolutions, and declarations discussed above.

The explicit reference to the right to water in the Constitution of the Republic of South Africa of 1996 offers a prime example of the gradual global recognition of the right to water.[293] Article 27 of the Constitution, dealing with health care, food, water, and social security, states that: "(1) Everyone has the right to have access to health care services, including reproductive health care; sufficient food and water; and social security, including, if they are unable to support themselves and their dependants, appropriate social assistance. (2) The state must take reasonable legislative and other measures, within its available resources, to achieve the progressive realisation of each of these rights."[294] The South African Water

---

[293] Constitution of the Republic of South Africa 1996 (Act No. 108 of 1996 entered into force February 4, 1997), in Albert Blaustein & Gisbert Flanz, eds., *supra* n. 216, in Vol. XVI, at 13.

[294] It should be noted that, like the ICESCR, the South African Constitution subjects this right to the available resources, and underscores the notion of progressive realization of the right. *See id.* Furthermore, Article 26 of the South African Constitution deals with the right to housing. That Article reads "(1) Everyone has the right to have access to adequate housing. (2) The state must take reasonable legislative and other measures, within its available resources, to achieve the progressive realization of this right." This article of the Constitution has been the subject of litigation before the South African Constitutional Court in the case of *Grootboom v. The Government of the Republic of South Africa, see supra* n. 183 and *see* <http://www.bday.co.za/bday/content/direct/0,3523,717355-6078-0,00.html>. In that case the Court ordered the government to rewrite its housing program to "provide relief for people who have no access to land, no roof over their heads and who are living in intolerable conditions or crisis situations." *See id.* The Court refused to simply accept the government's contention that it has taken reasonable measures within its available resources. Instead, the Court ordered the government to "set aside a reasonable portion of its budget for such relief." This is certainly a landmark decision as the Court has laid down the parameters of what the executive needs to do to meet its constitutional obligations. As has been noted by one observer, "the judgment has made a large contribution to the development of the jurisprudence on

Services Act, which entered into force nine months after the Constitution,[295] addresses the right to water in a number of provisions. Article 3 of the Act states that "everyone has a right of access to basic water supply and basic sanitation." The same Article requires every water services institution to take reasonable measures to realize these rights.[296] It also requires every water services authority to provide, in its water services development plans, for measures to realize these rights.[297] The Act lays down detailed procedures for the limitation or discontinuation of services, and stipulates that those procedures "must not result in a person being denied access to basic water services for non-payment, where that person proves, to the satisfaction of the relevant water services authority, that he or she is unable to pay for basic services."[298]

Similarly, the obligation under the Protocol on Water and Health requiring the States Parties to provide equitable access to water, adequate in terms both of

---

socio-economic rights and the nature of positive duties placed on the State to realize these rights. The judgment has also been hailed in international law circles for its use of international law and for its contribution to the development of a 'transnational consensus' on what exactly is required from a State to progressively realize a specific socio-economic right." *See* Kameshni Pillay, *Implementing Grootboom* <http://www.communitylawcentre.org.za/ser/esr2002/2002july_grootboom.php#grootboom.php>. *See* in this connection General Comment No. 7, The Right to adequate housing, *supra* n. 183.

[295] *See* Republic of South Africa, Water Services Act, Act 108 of 1997 (assented to on November 27, 1997). Since the issue of the right to water in South Africa is dealt with under the Water Service Act, the South Africa Water Act of 1998 (Act No. 36 of 1998) does not include any specific reference to the issue of the human right to water. However, Article 2 of the Act enumerates the purposes of the Act. The Article lays down 11 purposes, which include (a) meeting the basic human needs of present and future generations; (b) promoting equitable access to water; (c) redressing the results of past racial and gender discrimination; and (d) promoting the efficient, sustainable, and beneficial use of water in the public interests. Furthermore, Article 3 (2) endows the Minister of Water Affairs and Forests with ultimate responsibility for ensuring that "water is allocated equitably and used beneficially in the public interest, while promoting environmental values." For a general discussion of those issues, *see* Robyn Stein, *South Africa's New Democratic Water Legislation: National Government's Role as Public Trustee in Dam Building and Management Activities*, 18 Journal of Energy and Natural Resources Law 285 (2000).

[296] *See id.*, Article 3 (2). Article 1 (xxi) of the Water Services Act defines "water services institution" to mean a water services authority, a water services provider, a water board, and a water services committee.

[297] *See id.*, Article 3 (3). Article 1 (xx) of the Water Services Act defines "water services authority" to mean any municipality, including a district or rural council . . . responsible for ensuring access to water services.

[298] *See id.*, Article 4 (3) (c). Article 9 of the Water Services Act authorizes the Minister of Water Affairs and Forestry to prescribe the standards and tariffs for water services, taking into consideration, *inter alia,* the need for everyone to have reasonable quality of life as well as the need for equitable access to water services. In this connection, reference should be made to the *Manquele* case, *see supra* n. 262, which addressed the issue of the right to water. The case

quantity and quality, to all members of the population, represents another milestone in the direction of establishing the concept of the human right to water.[299] The recent decision of the European Court of Justice, which found both France and the United Kingdom in breach of certain obligations with regard to water quality under certain European directives, will assist in strengthening the legal basis for the human right to water.[300]

The resolution of the United Nations General Assembly reaffirming the right to food and clean water as fundamental human rights,[301] while without legally binding effect, bolsters General Comment No. 15. This is because the General

---

deals with Article 3 and Section 4 (3) of the Water Services Act. The applicant failed to pay for water in excess of the free six kilolitres per month provided by the Durban Transitional Metropolitan Council (DTMC). The DTMC, invoking its bylaws, gave the applicant written notice and allowed for representations to be made before disconnecting her water supply. The applicant argued that the bylaws were inconsistent with the Water Services Act because the disconnection resulted in her being denied access to basic water services while she was unable to pay for basic services. The Court noted that in Section 4 (3) of the Water Services Act, "basic water supply" is "the prescribed minimum standard of water supply services necessary for the reliable supply of a sufficient quantity and quality . . ." and that the term "prescribed" indicates that regulations made under the Act must give further content to the term "basic water supply." Since no such regulations exist, the Court indicated that the issue would concern policy matters that are outside the purview of the court. Furthermore, the court was satisfied that the procedures for disconnection under the bylaws were not inconsistent with the Water Services Act. Another factor cited by the court as a reason for its judgment was an earlier tampering of the applicant with the service during a previous disconnection. One of the questions asked in connection with this case is whether the decision of the court would have been different had the applicant based her arguments on the constitutional provisions on the right to water, rather than on the provisions of the Water Services Act.

[299] For the Protocol on Water and Health, *see supra* n. 233.

[300] *See* Case C-266/99 (1999/C- 281/06), *Commission v. French Republic* where the European Court of Justice found France to have failed in its obligations under Directive 75/440/EEC (O.J. L 145, 13.6.1977, at 1) concerning the quality required of surface waters intended for the abstraction of drinking water in Member States (also known as the Surface Water Directive), and in particular Article 4 thereof. The Commission's principal contention centered on France's failure to take necessary measures to ensure that water intended for abstraction of drinking water conform with the values laid down pursuant to Article 3, and the degradation of the quality of surface water by pollution caused by nitrates. Similarly, in Case 69/99 (1999/C 1999/069), *Commission v. United Kingdom*, the European Court of Justice found that the U.K. had failed to fulfill its obligations under Directive 91/676/EEC (OJ L 375, 31.12.1991) concerning protection of waters against pollution caused by nitrates from agricultural sources and the identification of waters affected by pollution. The U.K. had, in fact, omitted from consideration all surface and ground waters not being used for the extraction of drinking water, thus inappropriately limiting the areas. Since the decision, designation processes have been re-launched in England, Scotland, and Wales that could lead to around 80 percent of England being designated as Nitrate Vulnerable Zones (NVZ), which would demand that action programs be put in place. For more on this case *see* <http://europa.eu.int/comm/secretariat_general/sgb/droit_com/index_en.htm#infractions>.

[301] *See supra* n. 32.

Assembly has gone beyond approving reports of the Committee on Economic, Social and Cultural Rights on the right to water, and affirmed the right by a decisive and very visible action of its own.[302] This Resolution signaled clear endorsement by the General Assembly of the primordial importance of water to other rights. Similarly, the adoption of the Millennium Development Goals, which include reducing by half the proportion of people who have no access to safe drinking water by the year 2015, is another clear and unequivocal endorsement of the right to water by the United Nations General Assembly.[303]

Mention should also be made of the recent resolution of the General Assembly of the United Nations on the "International Decade for Action, 'Water for Life' 2005— 2015."[304] The Resolution recalled the General Assembly resolution declaring the year 2003 as the International Year of Freshwater,[305] as well as Agenda 21,[306] and the Johannesburg Plan of Implementation,[307] and emphasized that water is critical for sustainable development, including environmental integrity and the eradication of poverty and hunger, and is indispensable for human health and well-being. It reaffirmed the internationally agreed development goals on water and sanitation, including those contained in the Millennium Declaration,[308] and restated the determination to achieve the goal to halve, by the year 2015, the proportion of people who are unable to reach or to afford safe drinking water, as well as the goal to halve the proportion of people without basic access to sanitation. The Resolution proclaims the period from 2005 to 2015 as the International Decade for Action, 'Water for Life' commencing on World Water Day, March 22, 2005, and stated that the goals of the Decade would be a greater focus on water-related issues, at all levels, and on the implementation of water-related programs and projects to achieve the internationally agreed water-related goals.[309] It calls upon the relevant United Nations bodies, specialized

---

[302] *See id.*

[303] *See supra* n. 42.

[304] *See* General Assembly Resolution A/Res/58/217, adopted on December 23, 2003, *supra* n. 45.

[305] *See supra* n. 44.

[306] *See supra* n. 21.

[307] *See supra* n. 43.

[308] *See supra* n. 42.

[309] *See supra* n. 45, paragraphs 1 and 2.

agencies, regional commissions, and other organizations of the United Nations system to deliver a coordinated response to make the 'Water for Life' Decade, a decade for action.[310]

This Resolution strengthens the water-related goals of the Millennium Declaration by specifically focusing the attention of the world community on those goals during the decade 2005–2015. Although the Resolution is short of specific monitorable actions to achieve those goals, it should be viewed as another building block that should reinforce the notion of the human right to water, and assist in achieving such a goal.

Thus, it can be concluded that a number of legal instruments, as well as actions, at local, national, and international levels are emerging and reinforcing the recognition of the human right to water.

---

[310] *See supra* n. 45, paragraph 5.

CONCLUSION

The steady growth in world population, urbanization, and hydrological variability, along with the rampant spread of environmental degradation have all increased the pressure placed on the finite water resources available to mankind. This, in turn, has sharpened the competing demands for water, and prompted a rethinking of, and an extensive debate on, some of the basic issues related to water. The human right to water is one of the core issues of this debate, and has been on the global agenda since the 1970s. However, the resolutions and declarations that have been adopted since that time at the different United Nations conferences and other conferences and forums, have vacillated between declaring water a basic human need and a human right. It is in this context that General Comment No. 15, recognizing a human right to water, has its relevance and importance. Indeed, the Comment has heightened and energized this debate, adding both legal and policy dimensions.

The underlying thesis of this Study is that there exists in international law today an emerging human right to water. We identify that right in a variety of instruments, both international and domestic. In some of those instruments the right is provided for explicitly, in others implicitly; some are legally binding, and others remain largely aspirational. One conclusion we draw is that there is an evolving relationship between the "parallel" developments at the international and domestic levels, since both exist in a complex interrelationship, and are not mutually exclusive. Rather, they are complementary, such that they can all be viewed as supporting the emergence of a human right to water.

In articulating this thesis we have focused on developments related to the right to water that have occurred at three distinct, though we argue, intertwined, levels. First, and most importantly, are the developments at the level of international conventions. General Comment No. 15 was issued in the context of a legally binding treaty, the ICESCR, and the human right to water is recognized based on some of its provisions. Other treaties in this context include the Convention on the Rights of the Child as well as the International Convention on the Elimination of All Forms of Discrimination against Women. The second level is the propagation, over the last several decades, of a significant body of soft law on the right to water and on water as a vital need. This body of soft law includes the wide array of resolutions, declarations, and action plans of the different conferences and forums, as well as the resolutions of the United Nations General Assembly. Indeed, the Committee on Economic, Social and Cultural Rights reached as far back as the Universal Declaration of Human Rights and highlighted some of its provisions to argue for the recognition of the right to water. The third level concerns the developments that have occurred in parallel with the latter, at the level of domestic constitutions and legislation in some countries around the world establishing a human right to water.

Taking these levels of development in turn, we should first address General Comment No. 15, which remains the clearest and most explicit recognition of the human right to water in international law. While General Comments by the Committee cannot be said to create or even identify new rights, they are properly viewed as offering more than mere guidance to States Parties to the ICESCR. It is therefore critical to assess the potency of the General Comment in the context of this legally binding instrument, that is the ICESCR. The Comment should also be considered in the context of an institutional and procedural setting that gives it special significance and legitimacy. At the institutional setting, the gradual emergence of the Committee on Economic, Social and Cultural Rights from a mere group within the ECOSOC to a full-fledged independent body, akin to the Treaty body under the ICCPR, provides considerable legitimacy and weight to the General Comments this Committee issues. From the procedural and substantive points of view, and in the absence of an authoritative mechanism for settling potential disputes arising from divergent interpretations of the ICESCR's provisions, and given the dearth of commentary by States as to the meaning of the ICESCR's provisions, the practice of issuing General Comments has special legal significance and weight.

General Comment No.15 undoubtedly possesses the requisite elements for the recognition and clarification of the human right to water as part of the obligations of States Parties under the ICESCR. Indeed, as a substantive legal matter, the Committee has a duty to explain and elaborate economic, social, and cultural rights under the ICESCR for the States Parties, as well as the global community. This is one of the seminal roles of the Committee, and one of the fundamental purposes of General Comments.

It is worth noting that the General Comment is not limited to simply exhorting the States Parties to realize the right to water, but has grounded the right in three basic principles. The first of these principles is the derivation, or inference, of the right to water from Article 11 of the ICESCR regarding adequate standard of living, including food, as well as from Article 12 of the ICESCR regarding the enjoyment of the highest attainable standard of physical and mental health. The second principle is that of the centrality and necessity of water to other rights under the ICESCR, such as the right to adequate housing and food, and the right to life and liberty. The third principle is the prior recognition of the right in other declarations and resolutions, including those issued at Mar del Plata, Dublin, Rio, and in the Millennium Development Goals. They also include resolutions adopted by the General Assembly of the United Nations, and a number of conventions, including the Convention on the Rights of the Child, the Convention on the Elimination of All Forms of Discrimination against Women, as well as the United Nations Convention on the Law of the Non-Navigational Uses of International Watercourses. Prior recognition incorporates references made by the Committee to the right of water in earlier General Comments, such as General Comment No. 6 on the economic, social, and cultural rights of older persons.[311]

The second relevant level of international recognition of the right to water, after the above-quoted conventions, is that of soft law. This would include the different resolutions and declarations that have been adopted since the 1970s at the various United Nations and other conferences. The vacillation of those conferences, between declaring water as a basic human need or a human right, coupled with the fact that as declarations and resolutions these instruments do not possess formal binding effect, has resulted in their practical relevance being weak. Thus, while they undoubtedly have value as soft law, and while they may even have relevance so far as the emergence of principles of customary international law, they lack a clear "line of principle" or legal effect, and accordingly, do not bind *per se.*

General Comment No.15 has relevance in this connection, too, serving important "soft-law purposes" in addition to its clear legal purposes of direct relevance to the States Parties of the ICESCR outlined above. First, the General Comment

---

[311] It is indeed interesting to note the detail and rigor the Committee employed in its attempt to recognize and explain the right to water, which clearly indicates that the Committee has fully recognized the legal and practical implications of General Comment No. 15.

offers some significant measures of visibility of the right to water in the wider international context, as well as some definition and precision.[312] This is indeed due to the centrality of water to the other rights under the International Bill of Human Rights. In addition, the Comment offers renewed impetus to international organizations and civil society to coordinate and move forward with their efforts to translate soft law commitments at the domestic law level.

Similarly, General Comment No. 15 contributes to international momentum by offering considerable legal and moral support to the global efforts aimed at attaining the Millennium Development Goal related to water. The Comment should also buttress the two General Assembly resolutions on the Right to Development, one of which includes explicit references to the human right to water, as well as the resolution regarding the International Year of Freshwater. It should also strengthen and be strengthened by the General Assembly resolution on "International Decade for Action, 'Water for Life' 2005–2015," which proclaimed the main goal of the Decade as a greater focus on water-related issues in order to achieve the Millennium Development Goal related to water and sanitation by the year 2015. The shortcomings of the Comment discussed earlier, namely the suggestion that affordability could mean providing water free of charge, and the failure to address the issue of users' participation in the operation, management, and maintenance of water resources, as well as the failure to address the duties of those on whom the right is conferred, should in no way affect the legal or policy value of General Comment No. 15.

A third development that complements the two developments of conventions and soft law instruments, is the emerging recognition of the human right to water in domestic legal contexts in some countries, such as South Africa, Chile, and Armenia. The actions in those countries, such as the guarantee of a certain amount of water, or provision of water stamps, to a certain category of needy people, provide innovative examples of how the human right to water can be reflected in domestic regulatory frameworks. The significance of these domestic legal developments for the recognition and realization of the human right to water is

---

[312] Inasmuch as General Comment No. 15 has given visibility to the issue of the human right to water, water has also given a wider visibility to, and awareness of, the Committee on Economic, Social and Cultural Rights, and the General Comments it is issuing. This is attributed, no doubt, to the considerable attention being currently given, worldwide, to water resources issues.

important. First, they mirror, or at least reflect, in a complementary manner, the growing international consensus on the need to take legal action with respect to water resources, with special provision being made for the poor and vulnerable. Second, they are the actions of States effectuating obligations under the ICESCR and other more general "soft" international law commitments. In this regard, they set international precedents and provide general guidance for other states to emulate and replicate.

In conclusion, it is submitted that General Comment No. 15, recognizing a human right to water, provides further evidence that there is an incipient right to water evolving in public international law today. The General Comment derives this right from certain provisions of the ICESCR, thereby supporting the existence of an obligation on the part of the States Parties to the ICESCR to realize such a right. In this, the Comment buttresses the already voluminous body of soft law declarations and resolutions, as well as a growing number of domestic law provisions related to the human right to water. Perhaps even of greater significance is that General Comment No. 15 arguably heralds the emergence of a principle of international law on the human right to water.

Select Bibliography

Aït-Kadi, Mohamed, Aly Shady, & Andras Szöllösi-Nagy (eds.), *Water, the World's Common Heritage—Proceedings of the First World Water Forum, Marrakech, Morocco*, (Elsevier 1997).

Alston, Philip, *Out of the Abyss: The Challenges Confronting the New UN Committee on Economic, Social, and Cultural Rights,* 9 Hum. Rts. Q. 332 (1987).

———, *Establishing a right to petition under the Covenant on Economic, Social and Cultural Rights*, in *Collected Courses of the Academy of European Law: The Protection of Human Rights in Europe* Vol. IV, Book 2, 115 (Philip Alston & Bruno de Witte eds., European University Institute 1993).

———, *Economic and Social Rights*, in *Human Rights: An Agenda for the Next Century* 137 (Louis Henkin & John Lawrence Hargrove eds., The American Society of International Law 1994).

Alston, Philip, & Gerard Quinn, *The Nature and Scope of States Parties' Obligations under the International Covenant on Economic, Social and Cultural Rights*, 9 Hum. Rts. Q. 156 (1987).

American University International Law Review, *Reactions to the Report of the World Commission on Dams* (Special Edition, Volume 16, No. 6, 2001).

Bauer, Joanne R., & David A. Bell (eds.), *The East Asian Challenge for Human Rights* (Cambridge University Press 1999).

Brownlie, Ian, *Principles of Public International Law*, (5th ed., Oxford University Press 1998).

Buergenthal, Thomas, *International Human Rights in a Nutshell* (2d ed., West Pub. Co. 1995).

———, *The Normative and Institutional Evolution of International Human Rights* 19 Hum. Rts. Q. 703 (1997).

Caflisch, Lucius, *Regulation of the Uses of International Watercourses*, in *International Watercourses, Enhancing Cooperation and Managing Conflict,* 173 (Salman M. A. Salman & Laurence Boisson de Chazournes eds.) World Bank Technical Paper No. 414, Annex 1, (1998).

Caponera, Dante, *Water Laws in Moslem Countries*, FAO Irrigation and Drainage Papers No. 20, Vol 1, (Food and Agriculture Organization of the United Nations 1973).

————, *National and International Water Law and Administration, Selected Writings* (Kluwer Law International 2003).

Cassese, Antonio, *Human Rights in a Changing World* (Temple University Press 1990).

Chapman, Audrey, & Sage Russell (eds.), *Core Obligations: Building a Framework for Economic, Social and Cultural Rights* (Intersentia 2002).

Coomans F., & G. J. H. van Hoof (eds.), *The Right to Complain about Economic, Social and Cultural Rights: Proceedings of the Expert Meeting on the Adoption of an Optional Protocol to the International Covenant on Economic, Social and Cultural Rights* (Utrecht, January 25–28, 1995) (Netherlands Institute of Human Rights 1995).

Cosgrove, William J., & Frank R. Rijsberman, *World Water Vision—Making Water Everybody's Business* (World Water Council) (Earthscan 2000).

Cranston, Maurice, *What are Human Rights* (Taplinger Publishing Co. 1973).

Craven, Matthew, *Towards an unofficial petition procedure: A review of the role of the UN Committee on Economic, Social and Cultural Rights,* in *Social Rights as Human Rights: A European Challenge* 91 (Krzysztof Drzewicki, Catarina Krause, and Allan Rosas eds., Abo/Turku (Finland), Abo Akademi University, Institute for Human Rights 1994).

————, *The International Covenant on Economic, Social and Cultural Rights: A Perspective on its Development* (Clarendon Press 1995).

Dinstein, Yoram, *The Right to Life, Physical Integrity, and Liberty,* in *the International Bill of Rights: The Covenant on Civil and Political Rights*, (Louis Henkin ed., Columbia University Press 1981).

Donnelly, Jack, *The Concept of Human Rights* (Croom Helm 1985).

————, *International Human Rights* (Westview Press 1993).

————, *Universal Human Rights in Theory and Practice* (2d ed., Cornell University Press 2003).

Dupuy, Pierre-Marie, *Due Diligence in the International Law of Liability*, in *Legal Aspects of Transfrontier Pollution* (Organisation for Economic Cooperation and Development 1977).

Eide, Asbjørn, & Allan Rosas, *Economic, Social and Cultural Rights: A Universal Challenge,* in *Economic, Social and Cultural Rights, A Textbook* (Asbjørn Eide, Catarina Krause, & Allan Rosas eds., 2d ed., Martinus Nijhoff Publishers 2001).

Elver, Hilal, *Peaceful Uses of International Rivers—The Euphrates and Tigris Rivers Dispute* (Transnational Publishers Inc. 2002).

Etzioni, Amitai, *The New Golden Rule: Community and Morality in a Democratic Society* (Basic Books 1996).

Finnegan, William, *Letter from Bolivia—Leasing the Rain*, The New Yorker, April 8, 2002, at 43.

Gleick, Peter, *Basic Water Requirements for Human Activities: Meeting Basic Needs,* 21 Water International 82 (1996).

———, *The Human Right to Water*, 1 Water Policy 492 (1998).

Goodman, Louis, *Democracy, Sovereignty and Intervention,* 9(1) Am. U. J. of Int'l. Law and Policy 27 (1993).

Guerquin, François, Tarek Ahmed, Mi Hua, Tetsuya Ikeda, Vedat Ozbilen, and Marlies Schuttelaar, *World Water Actions, Making Water Flow for All* (Water Action Unit, World Water Council 2003).

Hague Academy of International Law, Centre for Studies and Research in International Law and International Relations, *Water Resources and International Law*, (Report of the 2001 Session by Salman M. A. Salman & Laurence Boisson de Chazournes) (Martinus Nijhoff Publishers 2002).

Handl, Günther, *Human Rights and Protection of the Environment: A Mildly 'Revisionist' View*, in *Human Rights, Sustainable Development and the Environment*, 117 (Antonio A. Cancado Trindade ed., Instituto Interamericano de Derechos Humanos and Banco Interamericano de Desarrollo 1995).

Hannum, Hurst, *The Status of the Universal Declaration of Human Rights in National and International Law*, 25 Ga. J. Int'l & Comp. L. 287 (1995–1996).

Hart, Herbert L. A., *The Concept of Law* (2d. ed., Oxford University Press 1994).

Henkin, Louis, *The Rights of Man Today* (Westview Press 1978).

———, *The International Bill of Rights* (Louis Henkin ed., Columbia University Press 1981).

———, *International Law: Politics, Values and Functions*, in *216 Collected Courses of the Hague Academy of International Law* Vol. IV (1989).

———, *Other 'Generations' of Rights*, in *International Law: Politics and Values* (Martinus Nijhoff Publishers 1995).

Hohmann, Harald, *Basic Documents of International Environmental Law* (Graham and Trotman 1992).

Khouri, Nadim, & Sarwat Chowdhury, *Mitigating Natural Groundwater Contamination in Bangladesh: Early Policy Lessons From a Development Project*, in *Groundwater—Legal and Policy Perspectives, Proceedings of a World Bank Seminar*, World Bank Technical Paper No. 456, 93 (Salman M. A. Salman ed., 1999).

Khushalani, Yougindra, *Human Rights in Asia and Africa* 4 H. R. L. J. 404 (1983).

Lawson, Edward, *Encyclopedia of Human Rights* (2d ed., Taylor and Francis 1996).

Lundqvist, Jan, *Rules and Roles in Water Policy and Management—Need for Clarification of Rights and Obligations*, 25 Water International 194 (2000).

Marasinghe, Lakshman, *Traditional conceptions of human rights in Africa*, in *Human Rights and Development in Africa* (C. Welch Jr. & R. Meltzer eds., State Univ. of New York Press 1984).

McCaffrey, Stephen, *A Human Right to Water: Domestic and International Implications*, 5 Geo. Intl. Envtl. L. Rev. 13 (1992).

———, *The UN Convention on the Law of the Non-Navigational Uses of International Watercourses: Prospects and Pitfalls*, in *International Watercourses, Enhancing Cooperation and Managing Conflict*, 173 (Salman M. A. Salman & Laurence Boisson de Chazournes eds.) World Bank Technical Paper No. 414, Annex 1 (1998).

———, *The Law of International Watercourses—Non-Navigational Uses* (Cambridge University Press 2001).

McGoldrick, Dominic, *The Human Rights Committee: Its Role in the Development of the International Covenant on Civil and Political Rights* (Clarendon Press 1991).

Meron, Theodor, *Human Rights Law-Making in the United Nations* (Oxford University Press 1986).

Morsink, Johannes, *The Philosophy of the Universal Declaration*, 6 Hum. Rts. Q. 309 (1989).

————, *The Universal Declaration of Human Rights: Origins, Drafting, and Intent (Pennsylvania Studies in Human Rights)* (University of Pennsylvania Press 1999).

Mutua, Makua, *Human Rights: A Political and Cultural Critique* (University of Pennsylvania Press 2002).

Newman, Frank, Joan Fitzpatrick, & David Weissbrodt, *International Human Rights: Law, Policy and Process* (3d ed., Anderson Publishing 2001).

Ramcharan, Bertrand, *The United Nations High Commissioner for Human Rights—The Challenges of International Protection* (Martinus Nijhoff Publishers 2002).

Raz, Joseph, *The Authority of Law: Essays on Law and Morality* (Oxford University Press 1979).

Robertson, A. H., & J. G. Merrils, *Human Rights in the World: An Introduction to the Study of the International Protection of Human Rights* (4th ed., Manchester University Press 1997).

Rodriguez-Rivera, Luis, *Is the Human Right to Environment Recognized Under International Law? It Depends on the Source*, 12 Colo. J. Int'l. Envtl. L. & Pol'y 1 (2001).

Salman, Salman M. A., *The Legal Framework for Water Users' Associations—A Comparative Study*, World Bank Technical Paper No. 360 (1997).

———— (ed.), *Groundwater—Legal and Policy Perspectives, Proceedings of a World Bank Seminar*, World Bank Technical Paper No. 456 (1999).

————, *The Abuja Ministerial Declaration—A Milestone or Just Another Statement?* 27 Water International 442 (2002).

————, *From Marrakech Through The Hague to Kyoto—Has the Global Debate on Water Reached a Dead End? Part One*, 28 Water International, 491 (2003); and *Part Two*, 29 Water International 11 (2004).

Salman, Salman M. A., & Laurence Boisson de Chazournes (eds.), *International Watercourses, Enhancing Cooperation and Managing Conflict,* 173 World Bank Technical Paper No. 414, Annex 1 (1998).

Salman, Salman M. A., & Kishor Uprety, *Conflict and Cooperation on South Asia's International Rivers—A Legal Perspective* (Kluwer Law International 2002).

Scott, Craig, *The Interdependence and Permeability of Human Rights Norms: Towards a Partial Fusion of the International Covenants on Human Rights* 27 Osgood Hall L. J. 769 (1989).

————, *Reaching Beyond (without abandoning) the Category of "Economic, Social and Cultural Rights"* 21 Hum. Rts. Q. 633 (1999).

Sen, Amartya, *Freedoms and Needs,* in The New Republic 31, 32 (January 10–17, 1994).

————, *Development as Freedom* (Alfred A. Knopf Inc. 1999).

Sengupta, Arjun, *The Right to Development as a Human Right* (Working Paper Series, François-Xavier Center for Health and Human Rights, Harvard University 1999).

Simma, Bruno, & Philip Alston, *The Sources of Human Rights Law: Custom, Jus Cogens and General Principles*, 12 Australian Yb. Int'l. L. 82 (1992).

Sohn, Louis B. (ed.) *Guide to Interpretation of the International Covenant on Economic, Social and Cultural Rights* Vols. I & II (Transnational Publishers 1994).

Stein, Robyn, *South Africa's New Democratic Water Legislation: National Government's Role as Public Trustee in Dam Building and Management Activities*, 18 Journal of Energy and Natural Resources Law 285 (2000).

Steiner, Henry J., & Philip Alston, *International Human Rights in Context: Law, Politics and Morals* (2d ed., Clarendon Press 2000).

Tanzi, Attila, & Maurizio Arcari, *The United Nations Convention on the Law of International Watercourses,* 38 (Kluwer Law International 2001).

United Nations, Report of the United Nations Water Conference, Mar del Plata, March 14–25, 1977, U.N. Publication, Sales No. E.77.II.A.12 (1977).

———, *Earth Summit, Agenda 21, The United Nations Programme of Action from Rio*, U.N. ISBN 92: 92-1-100509-4; Sales No. E.93.1.11, 166 (United Nations Publication 1993).

———, *1994 Yearbook of the International Law Commission* Vol. II, Part Two, 88 (United Nations Publications 1997).

United Nations Commission on Sustainable Development, *Comprehensive Assessment of Freshwater Resources of the World* (United Nations Publications 1997).

United Nations Economic and Social Council, Commission on Human Rights, Economic, Social and Cultural Rights, *Human Rights, Trade and Investment,* Report of the High Commissioner for Human Rights (E/CN.4/Sub.2/2003/9, July 3, 2003).

van Hoof, Godfried, *The Legal Nature of Economic, Social and Cultural Rights: A Rebuttal of Some Traditional Views,* in *The Right to Food,* 97 (Philip Alston & Katarina Tomaševski eds., Martinus Nijhoff Publishers 1984).

Vierdag, E.W., *The Legal Nature of Rights Granted by the International Covenant on Economic, Social and Cultural Rights* 9 Netherlands Yearbook of Int'l L. 69 (1978).

Welch, Claude E., & Virginia A. Leary (eds.), *Asian Perspectives on Human Rights* (Westview Press 1990).

World Bank, Water Resources Management Policy Paper (1993).

———, *Bolivia Water Management: A Tale of Three Cities*, World Bank Operations Evaluation Department, Précis Number 222 (Spring 2002).

———, *A Guide to the World Bank*, (The World Bank 2003).

World Commission for Water in the 21st Century, World Water Vision, Commission Report, *A Water Secure World: Vision for Water, Life and the Environment* 3 (2000).

World Commission on Dams, *Dams and Development—A New Framework for Decision-making (the Report of the World Commission on Dams)* (Earthscan Publications Ltd. 2000).

World Health Organization, *Right to Water (Health and Human Rights Publication Series, No. 3)* (World Health Organization 2003).

World Water Assessment Programme, *Water for People—Water for Life—The United Nations World Water Development Report* (UNESCO Publishing 2003).

World Water Council, Report of the World Panel on Financing Water Infrastructure, *Financing Water for All* (World Water Council 2003).

APPENDIXES

APPENDIX I
Universal Declaration of Human Rights

Adopted and proclaimed by General Assembly resolution 217 A (III) of 10 December 1948

On December 10, 1948, the General Assembly of the United Nations adopted and proclaimed the Universal Declaration of Human Rights, the full text of which appears in the following pages. Following this historic act the Assembly called upon all Member countries to publicize the text of the Declaration and "to cause it to be disseminated, displayed, read and expounded principally in schools and other educational institutions, without distinction based on the political status of countries or territories."

PREAMBLE

Whereas recognition of the inherent dignity and of the equal and inalienable rights of all members of the human family is the foundation of freedom, justice and peace in the world,

Whereas disregard and contempt for human rights have resulted in barbarous acts which have outraged the conscience of mankind, and the advent of a world in which human beings shall enjoy freedom of speech and belief and freedom from fear and want has been proclaimed as the highest aspiration of the common people,

Whereas it is essential, if man is not to be compelled to have recourse, as a last resort, to rebellion against tyranny and oppression, that human rights should be protected by the rule of law,

Whereas it is essential to promote the development of friendly relations between nations,

Whereas the peoples of the United Nations have in the Charter reaffirmed their faith in fundamental human rights, in the dignity and worth of the human person and in the equal rights of men and women and have determined to promote social progress and better standards of life in larger freedom,

Whereas Member States have pledged themselves to achieve, in co-operation with the United Nations, the promotion of universal respect for and observance of human rights and fundamental freedoms,

Whereas a common understanding of these rights and freedoms is of the greatest importance for the full realization of this pledge,

Now, Therefore,

The General Assembly

Proclaims this Universal Declaration of Human Rights as a common standard of achievement for all peoples and all nations, to the end that every individual and every organ of society, keeping this Declaration constantly in mind, shall strive by teaching and education to promote respect for these rights and freedoms and by progressive measures, national and international, to secure their universal and effective recognition and observance, both among the peoples of Member States themselves and among the peoples of territories under their jurisdiction.

Article 1

All human beings are born free and equal in dignity and rights. They are endowed with reason and conscience and should act towards one another in a spirit of brotherhood.

Article 2

Everyone is entitled to all the rights and freedoms set forth in this Declaration, without distinction of any kind, such as race, colour, sex, language, religion, political or other opinion, national or social origin, property, birth or other status.

Furthermore, no distinction shall be made on the basis of the political, jurisdictional or international status of the country or territory to which a person belongs, whether it be independent, trust, non-self-governing or under any other limitation of sovereignty.

Article 3

Everyone has the right to life, liberty and security of person.

Article 4

No one shall be held in slavery or servitude; slavery and the slave trade shall be prohibited in all their forms.

Article 5

No one shall be subjected to torture or to cruel, inhuman or degrading treatment or punishment.

Article 6

Everyone has the right to recognition everywhere as a person before the law.

Article 7

All are equal before the law and are entitled without any discrimination to equal protection of the law. All are entitled to equal protection against any discrimination in violation of this Declaration and against any incitement to such discrimination.

Article 8

Everyone has the right to an effective remedy by the competent national tribunals for acts violating the fundamental rights granted him by the constitution or by law.

Article 9

No one shall be subjected to arbitrary arrest, detention or exile.

Article 10

Everyone is entitled in full equality to a fair and public hearing by an independent and impartial tribunal, in the determination of his rights and obligations and of any criminal charge against him.

Article 11

1. Everyone charged with a penal offence has the right to be presumed innocent until proved guilty according to law in a public trial at which he has had all the guarantees necessary for his defence.

2. No one shall be held guilty of any penal offence on account of any act or omission which did not constitute a penal offence, under national or international law, at the time when it was committed. Nor shall a heavier penalty be imposed than the one that was applicable at the time the penal offence was committed.

Article 12

No one shall be subjected to arbitrary interference with his privacy, family, home or correspondence, nor to attacks upon his honour and reputation. Everyone has the right to the protection of the law against such interference or attacks.

Article 13

1. Everyone has the right to freedom of movement and residence within the borders of each state.

2. Everyone has the right to leave any country, including his own, and to return to his country.

Article 14

1. Everyone has the right to seek and to enjoy in other countries asylum from persecution.

2. This right may not be invoked in the case of prosecutions genuinely arising from non-political crimes or from acts contrary to the purposes and principles of the United Nations.

Article 15

1. Everyone has the right to a nationality.

2. No one shall be arbitrarily deprived of his nationality nor denied the right to change his nationality.

Article 16

1. Men and women of full age, without any limitation due to race, nationality or religion, have the right to marry and to found a family. They are entitled to equal rights as to marriage, during marriage and at its dissolution.

2. Marriage shall be entered into only with the free and full consent of the intending spouses.

3. The family is the natural and fundamental group unit of society and is entitled to protection by society and the State.

Article 17

1. Everyone has the right to own property alone as well as in association with others.

2. No one shall be arbitrarily deprived of his property.

Article 18

Everyone has the right to freedom of thought, conscience and religion; this right includes freedom to change his religion or belief, and freedom, either alone or in community with others and in public or private, to manifest his religion or belief in teaching, practice, worship and observance.

Article 19

Everyone has the right to freedom of opinion and expression; this right includes freedom to hold opinions without interference and to seek, receive and impart information and ideas through any media and regardless of frontiers.

Article 20

1. Everyone has the right to freedom of peaceful assembly and association.

2. No one may be compelled to belong to an association.

Article 21

1. Everyone has the right to take part in the government of his country, directly or through freely chosen representatives.

2. Everyone has the right of equal access to public service in his country.

3. The will of the people shall be the basis of the authority of government; this will shall be expressed in periodic and genuine elections which shall be by universal and equal suffrage and shall be held by secret vote or by equivalent free voting procedures.

Article 22

Everyone, as a member of society, has the right to social security and is entitled to realization, through national effort and international co-operation and in accordance with the organization and resources of each State, of the economic, social and cultural rights indispensable for his dignity and the free development of his personality.

Article 23

1. Everyone has the right to work, to free choice of employment, to just and favourable conditions of work and to protection against unemployment.

2. Everyone, without any discrimination, has the right to equal pay for equal work.

3. Everyone who works has the right to just and favourable remuneration ensuring for himself and his family an existence worthy of human dignity, and supplemented, if necessary, by other means of social protection.

4. Everyone has the right to form and to join trade unions for the protection of his interests.

Article 24

Everyone has the right to rest and leisure, including reasonable limitation of working hours and periodic holidays with pay.

Article 25

1. Everyone has the right to a standard of living adequate for the health and well-being of himself and of his family, including food, clothing, housing and medical care and necessary social services, and the right to security in the event of unemployment, sickness, disability, widowhood, old age or other lack of livelihood in circumstances beyond his control.

2. Motherhood and childhood are entitled to special care and assistance. All children, whether born in or out of wedlock, shall enjoy the same social protection.

Article 26

1. Everyone has the right to education. Education shall be free, at least in the elementary and fundamental stages. Elementary education shall be compulsory. Technical and professional education shall be made generally available and higher education shall be equally accessible to all on the basis of merit.

2. Education shall be directed to the full development of the human personality and to the strengthening of respect for human rights and fundamental freedoms. It shall promote understanding, tolerance and friendship among all nations, racial or religious groups, and shall further the activities of the United Nations for the maintenance of peace.

3. Parents have a prior right to choose the kind of education that shall be given to their children.

Article 27

1. Everyone has the right freely to participate in the cultural life of the community, to enjoy the arts and to share in scientific advancement and its benefits.

2. Everyone has the right to the protection of the moral and material interests resulting from any scientific, literary or artistic production of which he is the author.

Article 28

Everyone is entitled to a social and international order in which the rights and freedoms set forth in this Declaration can be fully realized.

Article 29

1. Everyone has duties to the community in which alone the free and full development of his personality is possible.

2. In the exercise of his rights and freedoms, everyone shall be subject only to such limitations as are determined by law solely for the purpose of securing due recognition and respect for the rights and freedoms of others and of meeting the just requirements of morality, public order and the general welfare in a democratic society.

3. These rights and freedoms may in no case be exercised contrary to the purposes and principles of the United Nations.

Article 30

Nothing in this Declaration may be interpreted as implying for any State, group or person any right to engage in any activity or to perform any act aimed at the destruction of any of the rights and freedoms set forth herein.

APPENDIX II
International Covenant on Economic, Social and Cultural Rights

Adopted and opened for signature, ratification and accession by General Assembly resolution 2200A (XXI) of 16 December 1966

Entered into force 3 January 1976

PREAMBLE

The States Parties to the present Covenant,

Considering that, in accordance with the principles proclaimed in the Charter of the United Nations, recognition of the inherent dignity and of the equal and inalienable rights of all members of the human family is the foundation of freedom, justice and peace in the world,

Recognizing that these rights derive from the inherent dignity of the human person,

Recognizing that, in accordance with the Universal Declaration of Human Rights, the ideal of free human beings enjoying freedom from fear and want can only be achieved if conditions are created whereby everyone may enjoy his economic, social and cultural rights, as well as his civil and political rights,

Considering the obligation of States under the Charter of the United Nations to promote universal respect for, and observance of, human rights and freedoms,

Realizing that the individual, having duties to other individuals and to the community to which he belongs, is under a responsibility to strive for the promotion and observance of the rights recognized in the present Covenant,

Agree upon the following articles:

PART I

Article 1

1. All peoples have the right of self-determination. By virtue of that right they freely determine their political status and freely pursue their economic, social and cultural development.

2. All peoples may, for their own ends, freely dispose of their natural wealth and resources without prejudice to any obligations arising out of international economic co-operation, based upon the principle of mutual benefit, and international law. In no case may a people be deprived of its own means of subsistence.

3. The States Parties to the present Covenant, including those having responsibility for the administration of Non-Self-Governing and Trust Territories, shall promote the realization of the right of self-determination, and shall respect that right, in conformity with the provisions of the Charter of the United Nations.

PART II

Article 2

1. Each State Party to the present Covenant undertakes to take steps, individually and through international assistance and co-operation, especially economic and technical, to the maximum of its available resources, with a view to achieving progressively the full realization of the rights recognized in the present Covenant by all appropriate means, including particularly the adoption of legislative measures.

2. The States Parties to the present Covenant undertake to guarantee that the rights enunciated in the present Covenant will be exercised without discrimination of any kind as to race, colour, sex, language, religion, political or other opinion, national or social origin, property, birth or other status.

3. Developing countries, with due regard to human rights and their national economy, may determine to what extent they would guarantee the economic rights recognized in the present Covenant to non-nationals.

Article 3

The States Parties to the present Covenant undertake to ensure the equal right of men and women to the enjoyment of all economic, social and cultural rights set forth in the present Covenant.

Article 4

The States Parties to the present Covenant recognize that, in the enjoyment of those rights provided by the State in conformity with the present Covenant, the State may subject such rights only to such limitations as are determined by law only in so far as this may be compatible with the nature of these rights and solely for the purpose of promoting the general welfare in a democratic society.

Article 5

1. Nothing in the present Covenant may be interpreted as implying for any State, group or person any right to engage in any activity or to perform any act aimed at the destruction of any of the rights or freedoms recognized herein, or at their limitation to a greater extent than is provided for in the present Covenant.

2. No restriction upon or derogation from any of the fundamental human rights recognized or existing in any country in virtue of law, conventions, regulations or custom shall be admitted on the pretext that the present Covenant does not recognize such rights or that it recognizes them to a lesser extent.

PART III

Article 6

1. The States Parties to the present Covenant recognize the right to work, which includes the right of everyone to the opportunity to gain his living by work which he freely chooses or accepts, and will take appropriate steps to safeguard this right.

2. The steps to be taken by a State Party to the present Covenant to achieve the full realization of this right shall include technical and vocational guidance and training programmes, policies and techniques to achieve steady economic, social and cultural development and full and productive employment under conditions safeguarding fundamental political and economic freedoms to the individual.

Article 7

The States Parties to the present Covenant recognize the right of everyone to the enjoyment of just and favourable conditions of work which ensure, in particular:

(a) Remuneration which provides all workers, as a minimum, with:

(i) Fair wages and equal remuneration for work of equal value without distinction of any kind, in particular women being guaranteed conditions of work not inferior to those enjoyed by men, with equal pay for equal work;

(ii) A decent living for themselves and their families in accordance with the provisions of the present Covenant;

(b) Safe and healthy working conditions;

(c) Equal opportunity for everyone to be promoted in his employment to an appropriate higher level, subject to no considerations other than those of seniority and competence;

(d) Rest, leisure and reasonable limitation of working hours and periodic holidays with pay, as well as remuneration for public holidays.

Article 8

1. The States Parties to the present Covenant undertake to ensure:

(a) The right of everyone to form trade unions and join the trade union of his choice, subject only to the rules of the organization concerned, for the promotion and protection of his economic and social interests. No restrictions may be placed on the exercise of this right other than those prescribed by law and which are necessary in a democratic society in the interests of national security or public order or for the protection of the rights and freedoms of others;

(b) The right of trade unions to establish national federations or confederations and the right of the latter to form or join international trade-union organizations;

(c) The right of trade unions to function freely subject to no limitations other than those prescribed by law and which are necessary in a democratic society in the interests of national security or public order or for the protection of the rights and freedoms of others;

(d) The right to strike, provided that it is exercised in conformity with the laws of the particular country.

2. This article shall not prevent the imposition of lawful restrictions on the exercise of these rights by members of the armed forces or of the police or of the administration of the State.

3. Nothing in this article shall authorize States Parties to the International Labour Organisation Convention of 1948 concerning Freedom of Association and Protection of the Right to Organize to take legislative measures which would prejudice, or apply the law in such a manner as would prejudice, the guarantees provided for in that Convention.

Article 9

The States Parties to the present Covenant recognize the right of everyone to social security, including social insurance.

Article 10

The States Parties to the present Covenant recognize that:

1. The widest possible protection and assistance should be accorded to the family, which is the natural and fundamental group unit of society, particularly for its establishment and while it is responsible for the care and education of dependent children. Marriage must be entered into with the free consent of the intending spouses.

2. Special protection should be accorded to mothers during a reasonable period before and after childbirth. During such period working mothers should be accorded paid leave or leave with adequate social security benefits.

3. Special measures of protection and assistance should be taken on behalf of all children and young persons without any discrimination for reasons of parentage or other conditions. Children and young persons should be protected from economic and social exploitation. Their employment in work harmful to their morals or health or dangerous to life or likely to hamper their normal development should be punishable by law. States should also set age limits below which the paid employment of child labour should be prohibited and punishable by law.

Article 11

1. The States Parties to the present Covenant recognize the right of everyone to an adequate standard of living for himself and his family, including adequate food, clothing and housing, and to the continuous improvement of living conditions. The States Parties will take appropriate steps to ensure the realization of

this right, recognizing to this effect the essential importance of international co-operation based on free consent.

2. The States Parties to the present Covenant, recognizing the fundamental right of everyone to be free from hunger, shall take, individually and through international co-operation, the measures, including specific programmes, which are needed:

> (a) To improve methods of production, conservation and distribution of food by making full use of technical and scientific knowledge, by disseminating knowledge of the principles of nutrition and by developing or reforming agrarian systems in such a way as to achieve the most efficient development and utilization of natural resources;

> (b) Taking into account the problems of both food-importing and food-exporting countries, to ensure an equitable distribution of world food supplies in relation to need.

Article 12

1. The States Parties to the present Covenant recognize the right of everyone to the enjoyment of the highest attainable standard of physical and mental health.

2. The steps to be taken by the States Parties to the present Covenant to achieve the full realization of this right shall include those necessary for:

> (a) The provision for the reduction of the stillbirth-rate and of infant mortality and for the healthy development of the child;

> (b) The improvement of all aspects of environmental and industrial hygiene;

> (c) The prevention, treatment and control of epidemic, endemic, occupational and other diseases;

> (d) The creation of conditions which would assure to all medical service and medical attention in the event of sickness.

Article 13

1. The States Parties to the present Covenant recognize the right of everyone to education. They agree that education shall be directed to the full development of the human personality and the sense of its dignity, and shall strengthen the

respect for human rights and fundamental freedoms. They further agree that education shall enable all persons to participate effectively in a free society, promote understanding, tolerance and friendship among all nations and all racial, ethnic or religious groups, and further the activities of the United Nations for the maintenance of peace.

2. The States Parties to the present Covenant recognize that, with a view to achieving the full realization of this right:

(a) Primary education shall be compulsory and available free to all;

(b) Secondary education in its different forms, including technical and vocational secondary education, shall be made generally available and accessible to all by every appropriate means, and in particular by the progressive introduction of free education;

(c) Higher education shall be made equally accessible to all, on the basis of capacity, by every appropriate means, and in particular by the progressive introduction of free education;

(d) Fundamental education shall be encouraged or intensified as far as possible for those persons who have not received or completed the whole period of their primary education;

(e) The development of a system of schools at all levels shall be actively pursued, an adequate fellowship system shall be established, and the material conditions of teaching staff shall be continuously improved.

3. The States Parties to the present Covenant undertake to have respect for the liberty of parents and, when applicable, legal guardians to choose for their children schools, other than those established by the public authorities, which conform to such minimum educational standards as may be laid down or approved by the State and to ensure the religious and moral education of their children in conformity with their own convictions.

4. No part of this article shall be construed so as to interfere with the liberty of individuals and bodies to establish and direct educational institutions, subject always to the observance of the principles set forth in paragraph I of this article and to the requirement that the education given in such institutions shall conform to such minimum standards as may be laid down by the State.

Article 14

Each State Party to the present Covenant which, at the time of becoming a Party, has not been able to secure in its metropolitan territory or other territories under its jurisdiction compulsory primary education, free of charge, undertakes, within two years, to work out and adopt a detailed plan of action for the progressive implementation, within a reasonable number of years, to be fixed in the plan, of the principle of compulsory education free of charge for all.

Article 15

1. The States Parties to the present Covenant recognize the right of everyone:

   (a) To take part in cultural life;

   (b) To enjoy the benefits of scientific progress and its applications;

   (c) To benefit from the protection of the moral and material interests resulting from any scientific, literary or artistic production of which he is the author.

2. The steps to be taken by the States Parties to the present Covenant to achieve the full realization of this right shall include those necessary for the conservation, the development and the diffusion of science and culture.

3. The States Parties to the present Covenant undertake to respect the freedom indispensable for scientific research and creative activity.

4. The States Parties to the present Covenant recognize the benefits to be derived from the encouragement and development of international contacts and co-operation in the scientific and cultural fields.

PART IV

Article 16

1. The States Parties to the present Covenant undertake to submit in conformity with this part of the Covenant reports on the measures which they have adopted and the progress made in achieving the observance of the rights recognized herein.

2. (a) All reports shall be submitted to the Secretary-General of the United Nations, who shall transmit copies to the Economic and Social Council for consideration in accordance with the provisions of the present Covenant;

(b) The Secretary-General of the United Nations shall also transmit to the specialized agencies copies of the reports, or any relevant parts therefrom, from States Parties to the present Covenant which are also members of these specialized agencies in so far as these reports, or parts therefrom, relate to any matters which fall within the responsibilities of the said agencies in accordance with their constitutional instruments.

Article 17

1. The States Parties to the present Covenant shall furnish their reports in stages, in accordance with a programme to be established by the Economic and Social Council within one year of the entry into force of the present Covenant after consultation with the States Parties and the specialized agencies concerned.

2. Reports may indicate factors and difficulties affecting the degree of fulfilment of obligations under the present Covenant.

3. Where relevant information has previously been furnished to the United Nations or to any specialized agency by any State Party to the present Covenant, it will not be necessary to reproduce that information, but a precise reference to the information so furnished will suffice.

Article 18

Pursuant to its responsibilities under the Charter of the United Nations in the field of human rights and fundamental freedoms, the Economic and Social Council may make arrangements with the specialized agencies in respect of their reporting to it on the progress made in achieving the observance of the provisions of the present Covenant falling within the scope of their activities. These reports may include particulars of decisions and recommendations on such implementation adopted by their competent organs.

Article 19

The Economic and Social Council may transmit to the Commission on Human Rights for study and general recommendation or, as appropriate, for information the reports concerning human rights submitted by States in accordance with articles 16 and 17, and those concerning human rights submitted by the specialized agencies in accordance with article 18.

Article 20

The States Parties to the present Covenant and the specialized agencies concerned may submit comments to the Economic and Social Council on any general recommendation under article 19 or reference to such general recommendation in any report of the Commission on Human Rights or any documentation referred to therein.

Article 21

The Economic and Social Council may submit from time to time to the General Assembly reports with recommendations of a general nature and a summary of the information received from the States Parties to the present Covenant and the specialized agencies on the measures taken and the progress made in achieving general observance of the rights recognized in the present Covenant.

Article 22

The Economic and Social Council may bring to the attention of other organs of the United Nations, their subsidiary organs and specialized agencies concerned with furnishing technical assistance any matters arising out of the reports referred to in this part of the present Covenant which may assist such bodies in deciding, each within its field of competence, on the advisability of international measures likely to contribute to the effective progressive implementation of the present Covenant.

Article 23

The States Parties to the present Covenant agree that international action for the achievement of the rights recognized in the present Covenant includes such methods as the conclusion of conventions, the adoption of recommendations, the furnishing of technical assistance and the holding of regional meetings and technical meetings for the purpose of consultation and study organized in conjunction with the Governments concerned.

Article 24

Nothing in the present Covenant shall be interpreted as impairing the provisions of the Charter of the United Nations and of the constitutions of the specialized agencies which define the respective responsibilities of the various organs of the United Nations and of the specialized agencies in regard to the matters dealt with in the present Covenant.

Article 25

Nothing in the present Covenant shall be interpreted as impairing the inherent right of all peoples to enjoy and utilize fully and freely their natural wealth and resources.

PART V

Article 26

1. The present Covenant is open for signature by any State Member of the United Nations or member of any of its specialized agencies, by any State Party to the Statute of the International Court of Justice, and by any other State which has been invited by the General Assembly of the United Nations to become a party to the present Covenant.

2. The present Covenant is subject to ratification. Instruments of ratification shall be deposited with the Secretary-General of the United Nations.

3. The present Covenant shall be open to accession by any State referred to in paragraph 1 of this article.

4. Accession shall be effected by the deposit of an instrument of accession with the Secretary-General of the United Nations.

5. The Secretary-General of the United Nations shall inform all States which have signed the present Covenant or acceded to it of the deposit of each instrument of ratification or accession.

Article 27

1. The present Covenant shall enter into force three months after the date of the deposit with the Secretary-General of the United Nations of the thirty-fifth instrument of ratification or instrument of accession.

2. For each State ratifying the present Covenant or acceding to it after the deposit of the thirty-fifth instrument of ratification or instrument of accession, the present Covenant shall enter into force three months after the date of the deposit of its own instrument of ratification or instrument of accession.

Article 28

The provisions of the present Covenant shall extend to all parts of federal States without any limitations or exceptions.

Article 29

1. Any State Party to the present Covenant may propose an amendment and file it with the Secretary-General of the United Nations. The Secretary-General shall thereupon communicate any proposed amendments to the States Parties to the present Covenant with a request that they notify him whether they favour a conference of States Parties for the purpose of considering and voting upon the proposals. In the event that at least one third of the States Parties favours such a conference, the Secretary-General shall convene the conference under the auspices of the United Nations. Any amendment adopted by a majority of the States Parties present and voting at the conference shall be submitted to the General Assembly of the United Nations for approval.

2. Amendments shall come into force when they have been approved by the General Assembly of the United Nations and accepted by a two-thirds majority of the States Parties to the present Covenant in accordance with their respective constitutional processes.

3. When amendments come into force they shall be binding on those States Parties which have accepted them, other States Parties still being bound by the provisions of the present Covenant and any earlier amendment which they have accepted.

Article 30

Irrespective of the notifications made under article 26, paragraph 5, the Secretary-General of the United Nations shall inform all States referred to in paragraph I of the same article of the following particulars:

(a) Signatures, ratifications and accessions under article 26;

(b) The date of the entry into force of the present Covenant under article 27 and the date of the entry into force of any amendments under article 29.

Article 31

1. The present Covenant, of which the Chinese, English, French, Russian and Spanish texts are equally authentic, shall be deposited in the archives of the United Nations.

2. The Secretary-General of the United Nations shall transmit certified copies of the present Covenant to all States referred to in article 26.

APPENDIX III
International Covenant on Civil and Political Rights*

Adopted and opened for signature, ratification and accession by General Assembly resolution 2200A (XXI) of 16 December 1966

Entered into force 23 March, 1976

PREAMBLE

The States Parties to the present Covenant,

Considering that, in accordance with the principles proclaimed in the Charter of the United Nations, recognition of the inherent dignity and of the equal and inalienable rights of all members of the human family is the foundation of freedom, justice and peace in the world,

Recognizing that these rights derive from the inherent dignity of the human person,

Recognizing that, in accordance with the Universal Declaration of Human Rights, the ideal of free human beings enjoying civil and political freedom and freedom from fear and want can only be achieved if conditions are created

---

* The Covenant has two Optional Protocols:

(i) The Optional Protocol to the International Covenant on Civil and Political Rights was adopted by General Assembly Resolution 2200A (XXI) of December 16, 1966. It entered into force on March 23, 1976, in accordance with Article 9, *see* 21 U.N. GAOR Supp. (No. 16) at 59, U.N. Doc. A/6316 (1966), 999 U.N.T.S. 302. As of March 2004, there were 113 signatories, of which 107 countries had ratified the instrument, *see* <http://untreaty.un.org/ENGLISH/bible/englishinternetbible/partI/chapterIV/treaty7.asp>.

(ii) The Second Optional Protocol to the International Covenant on Civil and Political Rights, aiming at the abolition of the death penalty, was adopted by the General Assembly Resolution A/Res/44/128 of December 15, 1989. It entered into force on July 11, 1991, *see* G.A. res. 44/128, annex, 44 U.N. GAOR Supp. (No. 49) at 207, U.N. Doc. A/44/49 (1989),1642 U.N.T.S. 414. As of March 2004, there were 60 signatories, of which 52 countries had ratified the instrument, *see* <http://untreaty.un.org/ENGLISH/bible/englishinternetbible/partI/chapterIV/treaty24.asp>.

whereby everyone may enjoy his civil and political rights, as well as his economic, social and cultural rights,

Considering the obligation of States under the Charter of the United Nations to promote universal respect for, and observance of, human rights and freedoms,

Realizing that the individual, having duties to other individuals and to the community to which he belongs, is under a responsibility to strive for the promotion and observance of the rights recognized in the present Covenant,

Agree upon the following articles:

PART I

Article I

1. All peoples have the right of self-determination. By virtue of that right they freely determine their political status and freely pursue their economic, social and cultural development.

2. All peoples may, for their own ends, freely dispose of their natural wealth and resources without prejudice to any obligations arising out of international economic co-operation, based upon the principle of mutual benefit, and international law. In no case may a people be deprived of its own means of subsistence.

3. The States Parties to the present Covenant, including those having responsibility for the administration of Non-Self-Governing and Trust Territories, shall promote the realization of the right of self-determination, and shall respect that right, in conformity with the provisions of the Charter of the United Nations.

PART II

Article 2

1. Each State Party to the present Covenant undertakes to respect and to ensure to all individuals within its territory and subject to its jurisdiction the rights recognized in the present Covenant, without distinction of any kind, such as race, colour, sex, language, religion, political or other opinion, national or social origin, property, birth or other status.

2. Where not already provided for by existing legislative or other measures, each State Party to the present Covenant undertakes to take the necessary steps, in accordance with its constitutional processes and with the provisions of the pre-

sent Covenant, to adopt such legislative or other measures as may be necessary to give effect to the rights recognized in the present Covenant.

3. Each State Party to the present Covenant undertakes:

(a) To ensure that any person whose rights or freedoms as herein recognized are violated shall have an effective remedy, notwithstanding that the violation has been committed by persons acting in an official capacity;

(b) To ensure that any person claiming such a remedy shall have his right thereto determined by competent judicial, administrative or legislative authorities, or by any other competent authority provided for by the legal system of the State, and to develop the possibilities of judicial remedy;

(c) To ensure that the competent authorities shall enforce such remedies when granted.

Article 3

The States Parties to the present Covenant undertake to ensure the equal right of men and women to the enjoyment of all civil and political rights set forth in the present Covenant.

Article 4

1. In time of public emergency which threatens the life of the nation and the existence of which is officially proclaimed, the States Parties to the present Covenant may take measures derogating from their obligations under the present Covenant to the extent strictly required by the exigencies of the situation, provided that such measures are not inconsistent with their other obligations under international law and do not involve discrimination solely on the ground of race, colour, sex, language, religion or social origin.

2. No derogation from articles 6, 7, 8 (paragraphs 1 and 2), 11, 15, 16 and 18 may be made under this provision.

3. Any State Party to the present Covenant availing itself of the right of derogation shall immediately inform the other States Parties to the present Covenant, through the intermediary of the Secretary-General of the United Nations, of the provisions from which it has derogated and of the reasons by which it was actuated. A further communication shall be made, through the same intermediary, on the date on which it terminates such derogation.

Article 5

1. Nothing in the present Covenant may be interpreted as implying for any State, group or person any right to engage in any activity or perform any act aimed at the destruction of any of the rights and freedoms recognized herein or at their limitation to a greater extent than is provided for in the present Covenant.

2. There shall be no restriction upon or derogation from any of the fundamental human rights recognized or existing in any State Party to the present Covenant pursuant to law, conventions, regulations or custom on the pretext that the present Covenant does not recognize such rights or that it recognizes them to a lesser extent.

PART III

Article 6

1. Every human being has the inherent right to life. This right shall be protected by law. No one shall be arbitrarily deprived of his life.

2. In countries which have not abolished the death penalty, sentence of death may be imposed only for the most serious crimes in accordance with the law in force at the time of the commission of the crime and not contrary to the provisions of the present Covenant and to the Convention on the Prevention and Punishment of the Crime of Genocide. This penalty can only be carried out pursuant to a final judgement rendered by a competent court.

3. When deprivation of life constitutes the crime of genocide, it is understood that nothing in this article shall authorize any State Party to the present Covenant to derogate in any way from any obligation assumed under the provisions of the Convention on the Prevention and Punishment of the Crime of Genocide.

4. Anyone sentenced to death shall have the right to seek pardon or commutation of the sentence. Amnesty, pardon or commutation of the sentence of death may be granted in all cases.

5. Sentence of death shall not be imposed for crimes committed by persons below eighteen years of age and shall not be carried out on pregnant women.

6. Nothing in this article shall be invoked to delay or to prevent the abolition of capital punishment by any State Party to the present Covenant.

Article 7

No one shall be subjected to torture or to cruel, inhuman or degrading treatment or punishment. In particular, no one shall be subjected without his free consent to medical or scientific experimentation.

Article 8

1. No one shall be held in slavery; slavery and the slave-trade in all their forms shall be prohibited.

2. No one shall be held in servitude.

3. (a) No one shall be required to perform forced or compulsory labour;

(b) Paragraph 3 (a) shall not be held to preclude, in countries where imprisonment with hard labour may be imposed as a punishment for a crime, the performance of hard labour in pursuance of a sentence to such punishment by a competent court;

(c) For the purpose of this paragraph the term "forced or compulsory labour" shall not include:

(i) Any work or service, not referred to in subparagraph (b), normally required of a person who is under detention in consequence of a lawful order of a court, or of a person during conditional release from such detention;

(ii) Any service of a military character and, in countries where conscientious objection is recognized, any national service required by law of conscientious objectors;

(iii) Any service exacted in cases of emergency or calamity threatening the life or well-being of the community;

(iv) Any work or service which forms part of normal civil obligations.

Article 9

1. Everyone has the right to liberty and security of person. No one shall be subjected to arbitrary arrest or detention. No one shall be deprived of his liberty except on such grounds and in accordance with such procedure as are established by law.

2. Anyone who is arrested shall be informed, at the time of arrest, of the reasons for his arrest and shall be promptly informed of any charges against him.

3. Anyone arrested or detained on a criminal charge shall be brought promptly before a judge or other officer authorized by law to exercise judicial power and shall be entitled to trial within a reasonable time or to release. It shall not be the general rule that persons awaiting trial shall be detained in custody, but release may be subject to guarantees to appear for trial, at any other stage of the judicial proceedings, and, should occasion arise, for execution of the judgement.

4. Anyone who is deprived of his liberty by arrest or detention shall be entitled to take proceedings before a court, in order that court may decide without delay on the lawfulness of his detention and order his release if the detention is not lawful.

5. Anyone who has been the victim of unlawful arrest or detention shall have an enforceable right to compensation.

Article 10

1. All persons deprived of their liberty shall be treated with humanity and with respect for the inherent dignity of the human person.

2. (a) Accused persons shall, save in exceptional circumstances, be segregated from convicted persons and shall be subject to separate treatment appropriate to their status as unconvicted persons;

    (b) Accused juvenile persons shall be separated from adults and brought as speedily as possible for adjudication.

3. The penitentiary system shall comprise treatment of prisoners the essential aim of which shall be their reformation and social rehabilitation. Juvenile offenders shall be segregated from adults and be accorded treatment appropriate to their age and legal status.

Article 11

No one shall be imprisoned merely on the ground of inability to fulfil a contractual obligation.

Article 12

1. Everyone lawfully within the territory of a State shall, within that territory, have the right to liberty of movement and freedom to choose his residence.

2. Everyone shall be free to leave any country, including his own.

3. The above-mentioned rights shall not be subject to any restrictions except those which are provided by law, are necessary to protect national security, public order (*ordre public*), public health or morals or the rights and freedoms of others, and are consistent with the other rights recognized in the present Covenant.

4. No one shall be arbitrarily deprived of the right to enter his own country.

Article 13

An alien lawfully in the territory of a State Party to the present Covenant may be expelled therefrom only in pursuance of a decision reached in accordance with law and shall, except where compelling reasons of national security otherwise require, be allowed to submit the reasons against his expulsion and to have his case reviewed by, and be represented for the purpose before, the competent authority or a person or persons especially designated by the competent authority.

Article 14

1. All persons shall be equal before the courts and tribunals. In the determination of any criminal charge against him, or of his rights and obligations in a suit at law, everyone shall be entitled to a fair and public hearing by a competent, independent and impartial tribunal established by law. The press and the public may be excluded from all or part of a trial for reasons of morals, public order (*ordre public*) or national security in a democratic society, or when the interest of the private lives of the parties so requires, or to the extent strictly necessary in the opinion of the court in special circumstances where publicity would prejudice the interests of justice; but any judgement rendered in a criminal case or in a suit at law shall be made public except where the interest of juvenile persons otherwise requires or the proceedings concern matrimonial disputes or the guardianship of children.

2. Everyone charged with a criminal offence shall have the right to be presumed innocent until proved guilty according to law.

3. In the determination of any criminal charge against him, everyone shall be entitled to the following minimum guarantees, in full equality:

(a) To be informed promptly and in detail in a language which he understands of the nature and cause of the charge against him;

(b) To have adequate time and facilities for the preparation of his defence and to communicate with counsel of his own choosing;

(c) To be tried without undue delay;

(d) To be tried in his presence, and to defend himself in person or through legal assistance of his own choosing; to be informed, if he does not have legal assistance, of this right; and to have legal assistance assigned to him, in any case where the interests of justice so require, and without payment by him in any such case if he does not have sufficient means to pay for it;

(e) To examine, or have examined, the witnesses against him and to obtain the attendance and examination of witnesses on his behalf under the same conditions as witnesses against him;

(f) To have the free assistance of an interpreter if he cannot understand or speak the language used in court;

(g) Not to be compelled to testify against himself or to confess guilt.

4. In the case of juvenile persons, the procedure shall be such as will take account of their age and the desirability of promoting their rehabilitation.

5. Everyone convicted of a crime shall have the right to his conviction and sentence being reviewed by a higher tribunal according to law.

6. When a person has by a final decision been convicted of a criminal offence and when subsequently his conviction has been reversed or he has been pardoned on the ground that a new or newly discovered fact shows conclusively that there has been a miscarriage of justice, the person who has suffered punishment as a result of such conviction shall be compensated according to law, unless it is proved that the non-disclosure of the unknown fact in time is wholly or partly attributable to him.

7. No one shall be liable to be tried or punished again for an offence for which he has already been finally convicted or acquitted in accordance with the law and penal procedure of each country.

Article 15

1. No one shall be held guilty of any criminal offence on account of any act or omission which did not constitute a criminal offence, under national or international law, at the time when it was committed. Nor shall a heavier penalty be

imposed than the one that was applicable at the time when the criminal offence was committed. If, subsequent to the commission of the offence, provision is made by law for the imposition of the lighter penalty, the offender shall benefit thereby.

2. Nothing in this article shall prejudice the trial and punishment of any person for any act or omission which, at the time when it was committed, was criminal according to the general principles of law recognized by the community of nations.

Article 16

Everyone shall have the right to recognition everywhere as a person before the law.

Article 17

1. No one shall be subjected to arbitrary or unlawful interference with his privacy, family, home or correspondence, nor to unlawful attacks on his honour and reputation.

2. Everyone has the right to the protection of the law against such interference or attacks.

Article 18

1. Everyone shall have the right to freedom of thought, conscience and religion. This right shall include freedom to have or to adopt a religion or belief of his choice, and freedom, either individually or in community with others and in public or private, to manifest his religion or belief in worship, observance, practice and teaching.

2. No one shall be subject to coercion which would impair his freedom to have or to adopt a religion or belief of his choice.

3. Freedom to manifest one's religion or beliefs may be subject only to such limitations as are prescribed by law and are necessary to protect public safety, order, health, or morals or the fundamental rights and freedoms of others.

4. The States Parties to the present Covenant undertake to have respect for the liberty of parents and, when applicable, legal guardians to ensure the religious and moral education of their children in conformity with their own convictions.

Article 19

1. Everyone shall have the right to hold opinions without interference.

2. Everyone shall have the right to freedom of expression; this right shall include freedom to seek, receive and impart information and ideas of all kinds, regardless of frontiers, either orally, in writing or in print, in the form of art, or through any other media of his choice.

3. The exercise of the rights provided for in paragraph 2 of this article carries with it special duties and responsibilities. It may therefore be subject to certain restrictions, but these shall only be such as are provided by law and are necessary:

(a) For respect of the rights or reputations of others;

(b) For the protection of national security or of public order (*ordre public*), or of public health or morals.

Article 20

1. Any propaganda for war shall be prohibited by law.

2. Any advocacy of national, racial or religious hatred that constitutes incitement to discrimination, hostility or violence shall be prohibited by law.

Article 21

The right of peaceful assembly shall be recognized. No restrictions may be placed on the exercise of this right other than those imposed in conformity with the law and which are necessary in a democratic society in the interests of national security or public safety, public order (*ordre public*), the protection of public health or morals or the protection of the rights and freedoms of others.

Article 22

1. Everyone shall have the right to freedom of association with others, including the right to form and join trade unions for the protection of his interests.

2. No restrictions may be placed on the exercise of this right other than those which are prescribed by law and which are necessary in a democratic society in the interests of national security or public safety, public order (*ordre public*), the protection of public health or morals or the protection of the rights and freedoms of others. This article shall not prevent the imposition of lawful restrictions on members of the armed forces and of the police in their exercise of this right.

3. Nothing in this article shall authorize States Parties to the International Labour Organisation Convention of 1948 concerning Freedom of Association and Protection of the Right to Organize to take legislative measures which would prejudice, or to apply the law in such a manner as to prejudice, the guarantees provided for in that Convention.

Article 23

1. The family is the natural and fundamental group unit of society and is entitled to protection by society and the State.

2. The right of men and women of marriageable age to marry and to found a family shall be recognized.

3. No marriage shall be entered into without the free and full consent of the intending spouses.

4. States Parties to the present Covenant shall take appropriate steps to ensure equality of rights and responsibilities of spouses as to marriage, during marriage and at its dissolution. In the case of dissolution, provision shall be made for the necessary protection of any children.

Article 24

1. Every child shall have, without any discrimination as to race, colour, sex, language, religion, national or social origin, property or birth, the right to such measures of protection as are required by his status as a minor, on the part of his family, society and the State.

2. Every child shall be registered immediately after birth and shall have a name.

3. Every child has the right to acquire a nationality.

Article 25

Every citizen shall have the right and the opportunity, without any of the distinctions mentioned in article 2 and without unreasonable restrictions:

(a) To take part in the conduct of public affairs, directly or through freely chosen representatives;

(b) To vote and to be elected at genuine periodic elections which shall be by universal and equal suffrage and shall be held by secret ballot, guaranteeing the free expression of the will of the electors;

(c) To have access, on general terms of equality, to public service in his country.

Article 26

All persons are equal before the law and are entitled without any discrimination to the equal protection of the law. In this respect, the law shall prohibit any discrimination and guarantee to all persons equal and effective protection against discrimination on any ground such as race, colour, sex, language, religion, political or other opinion, national or social origin, property, birth or other status.

Article 27

In those States in which ethnic, religious or linguistic minorities exist, persons belonging to such minorities shall not be denied the right, in community with the other members of their group, to enjoy their own culture, to profess and practise their own religion, or to use their own language.

PART IV

Article 28

1. There shall be established a Human Rights Committee (hereafter referred to in the present Covenant as the Committee). It shall consist of eighteen members and shall carry out the functions hereinafter provided.

2. The Committee shall be composed of nationals of the States Parties to the present Covenant who shall be persons of high moral character and recognized competence in the field of human rights, consideration being given to the usefulness of the participation of some persons having legal experience.

3. The members of the Committee shall be elected and shall serve in their personal capacity.

Article 29

1 . The members of the Committee shall be elected by secret ballot from a list of persons possessing the qualifications prescribed in article 28 and nominated for the purpose by the States Parties to the present Covenant.

2. Each State Party to the present Covenant may nominate not more than two persons. These persons shall be nationals of the nominating State.

3. A person shall be eligible for renomination.

Article 30

1. The initial election shall be held no later than six months after the date of the entry into force of the present Covenant.

2. At least four months before the date of each election to the Committee, other than an election to fill a vacancy declared in accordance with article 34, the Secretary-General of the United Nations shall address a written invitation to the States Parties to the present Covenant to submit their nominations for membership of the Committee within three months.

3. The Secretary-General of the United Nations shall prepare a list in alphabetical order of all the persons thus nominated, with an indication of the States Parties which have nominated them, and shall submit it to the States Parties to the present Covenant no later than one month before the date of each election.

4. Elections of the members of the Committee shall be held at a meeting of the States Parties to the present Covenant convened by the Secretary General of the United Nations at the Headquarters of the United Nations. At that meeting, for which two thirds of the States Parties to the present Covenant shall constitute a quorum, the persons elected to the Committee shall be those nominees who obtain the largest number of votes and an absolute majority of the votes of the representatives of States Parties present and voting.

Article 31

1. The Committee may not include more than one national of the same State.

2. In the election of the Committee, consideration shall be given to equitable geographical distribution of membership and to the representation of the different forms of civilization and of the principal legal systems.

Article 32

1. The members of the Committee shall be elected for a term of four years. They shall be eligible for re-election if renominated. However, the terms of nine of the members elected at the first election shall expire at the end of two years; immediately after the first election, the names of these nine members shall be chosen by lot by the Chairman of the meeting referred to in article 30, paragraph 4.

2. Elections at the expiry of office shall be held in accordance with the preceding articles of this part of the present Covenant.

Article 33

1. If, in the unanimous opinion of the other members, a member of the Committee has ceased to carry out his functions for any cause other than absence of a temporary character, the Chairman of the Committee shall notify the Secretary-General of the United Nations, who shall then declare the seat of that member to be vacant.

2. In the event of the death or the resignation of a member of the Committee, the Chairman shall immediately notify the Secretary-General of the United Nations, who shall declare the seat vacant from the date of death or the date on which the resignation takes effect.

Article 34

1. When a vacancy is declared in accordance with article 33 and if the term of office of the member to be replaced does not expire within six months of the declaration of the vacancy, the Secretary-General of the United Nations shall notify each of the States Parties to the present Covenant, which may within two months submit nominations in accordance with article 29 for the purpose of filling the vacancy.

2. The Secretary-General of the United Nations shall prepare a list in alphabetical order of the persons thus nominated and shall submit it to the States Parties to the present Covenant. The election to fill the vacancy shall then take place in accordance with the relevant provisions of this part of the present Covenant.

3. A member of the Committee elected to fill a vacancy declared in accordance with article 33 shall hold office for the remainder of the term of the member who vacated the seat on the Committee under the provisions of that article.

Article 35

The members of the Committee shall, with the approval of the General Assembly of the United Nations, receive emoluments from United Nations resources on such terms and conditions as the General Assembly may decide, having regard to the importance of the Committee's responsibilities.

Article 36

The Secretary-General of the United Nations shall provide the necessary staff and facilities for the effective performance of the functions of the Committee under the present Covenant.

Article 37

1. The Secretary-General of the United Nations shall convene the initial meeting of the Committee at the Headquarters of the United Nations.

2. After its initial meeting, the Committee shall meet at such times as shall be provided in its rules of procedure.

3. The Committee shall normally meet at the Headquarters of the United Nations or at the United Nations Office at Geneva.

Article 38

Every member of the Committee shall, before taking up his duties, make a solemn declaration in open committee that he will perform his functions impartially and conscientiously.

Article 39

1. The Committee shall elect its officers for a term of two years. They may be re-elected.

2. The Committee shall establish its own rules of procedure, but these rules shall provide, *inter alia*, that:

(a) Twelve members shall constitute a quorum;

(b) Decisions of the Committee shall be made by a majority vote of the members present.

Article 40

1. The States Parties to the present Covenant undertake to submit reports on the measures they have adopted which give effect to the rights recognized herein and on the progress made in the enjoyment of those rights:

(a) Within one year of the entry into force of the present Covenant for the States Parties concerned;

(b) Thereafter whenever the Committee so requests.

2. All reports shall be submitted to the Secretary-General of the United Nations, who shall transmit them to the Committee for consideration. Reports shall indicate the factors and difficulties, if any, affecting the implementation of the present Covenant.

3. The Secretary-General of the United Nations may, after consultation with the Committee, transmit to the specialized agencies concerned copies of such parts of the reports as may fall within their field of competence.

4. The Committee shall study the reports submitted by the States Parties to the present Covenant. It shall transmit its reports, and such general comments as it may consider appropriate, to the States Parties. The Committee may also transmit to the Economic and Social Council these comments along with the copies of the reports it has received from States Parties to the present Covenant.

5. The States Parties to the present Covenant may submit to the Committee observations on any comments that may be made in accordance with paragraph 4 of this article.

Article 41

1. A State Party to the present Covenant may at any time declare under this article that it recognizes the competence of the Committee to receive and consider communications to the effect that a State Party claims that another State Party is not fulfilling its obligations under the present Covenant. Communications under this article may be received and considered only if submitted by a State Party which has made a declaration recognizing in regard to itself the competence of the Committee. No communication shall be received by the Committee if it concerns a State Party which has not made such a declaration. Communications received under this article shall be dealt with in accordance with the following procedure:

(a) If a State Party to the present Covenant considers that another State Party is not giving effect to the provisions of the present Covenant, it may, by written communication, bring the matter to the attention of that State Party. Within three months after the receipt of the communication the receiving State shall afford the State which sent the communication an explanation, or any other statement in writing clarifying the matter which should include, to the extent possible and pertinent, reference to domestic procedures and remedies taken, pending, or available in the matter;

(b) If the matter is not adjusted to the satisfaction of both States Parties concerned within six months after the receipt by the receiving State of the initial communication, either State shall have the right to refer the matter to the Committee, by notice given to the Committee and to the other State;

(c) The Committee shall deal with a matter referred to it only after it has ascertained that all available domestic remedies have been invoked and exhausted in the matter, in conformity with the generally recognized principles of international law. This shall not be the rule where the application of the remedies is unreasonably prolonged;

(d) The Committee shall hold closed meetings when examining communications under this article;

(e) Subject to the provisions of subparagraph (c), the Committee shall make available its good offices to the States Parties concerned with a view to a friendly solution of the matter on the basis of respect for human rights and fundamental freedoms as recognized in the present Covenant;

(f) In any matter referred to it, the Committee may call upon the States Parties concerned, referred to in subparagraph (b), to supply any relevant information;

(g) The States Parties concerned, referred to in subparagraph (b), shall have the right to be represented when the matter is being considered in the Committee and to make submissions orally and/or in writing;

(h) The Committee shall, within twelve months after the date of receipt of notice under subparagraph (b), submit a report:

(i) If a solution within the terms of subparagraph (e) is reached, the Committee shall confine its report to a brief statement of the facts and of the solution reached;

(ii) If a solution within the terms of subparagraph (e) is not reached, the Committee shall confine its report to a brief statement of the facts; the written submissions and record of the oral submissions made by the States Parties concerned shall be attached to the report. In every matter, the report shall be communicated to the States Parties concerned.

2. The provisions of this article shall come into force when ten States Parties to the present Covenant have made declarations under paragraph I of this article. Such declarations shall be deposited by the States Parties with the Secretary-General of the United Nations, who shall transmit copies thereof to the other States Parties. A declaration may be withdrawn at any time by notification to the Secretary-General. Such a withdrawal shall not prejudice the consideration of any matter which is the subject of a communication already transmitted under this article; no further communication by any State Party shall be received after the notification of withdrawal of the declaration has been received by the Secretary-General, unless the State Party concerned has made a new declaration.

Article 42

1. (a) If a matter referred to the Committee in accordance with article 41 is not resolved to the satisfaction of the States Parties concerned, the Committee may, with the prior consent of the States Parties concerned, appoint an ad hoc Conciliation Commission (hereinafter referred to as the Commission). The good offices of the Commission shall be made available to the States Parties concerned with a view to an amicable solution of the matter on the basis of respect for the present Covenant;

    (b) The Commission shall consist of five persons acceptable to the States Parties concerned. If the States Parties concerned fail to reach agreement within three months on all or part of the composition of the Commission, the members of the Commission concerning whom no agreement has been reached shall be elected by secret ballot by a two-thirds majority vote of the Committee from among its members.

2. The members of the Commission shall serve in their personal capacity. They shall not be nationals of the States Parties concerned, or of a State not Party to the present Covenant, or of a State Party which has not made a declaration under article 41.

3. The Commission shall elect its own Chairman and adopt its own rules of procedure.

4. The meetings of the Commission shall normally be held at the Headquarters of the United Nations or at the United Nations Office at Geneva. However, they may be held at such other convenient places as the Commission may determine

in consultation with the Secretary-General of the United Nations and the States Parties concerned.

5. The secretariat provided in accordance with article 36 shall also service the commissions appointed under this article.

6. The information received and collated by the Committee shall be made available to the Commission and the Commission may call upon the States Parties concerned to supply any other relevant information.

7. When the Commission has fully considered the matter, but in any event not later than twelve months after having been seized of the matter, it shall submit to the Chairman of the Committee a report for communication to the States Parties concerned:

> (a) If the Commission is unable to complete its consideration of the matter within twelve months, it shall confine its report to a brief statement of the status of its consideration of the matter;

> (b) If an amicable solution to the matter on the basis of respect for human rights as recognized in the present Covenant is reached, the Commission shall confine its report to a brief statement of the facts and of the solution reached;

> (c) If a solution within the terms of subparagraph (b) is not reached, the Commission's report shall embody its findings on all questions of fact relevant to the issues between the States Parties concerned, and its views on the possibilities of an amicable solution of the matter. This report shall also contain the written submissions and a record of the oral submissions made by the States Parties concerned;

> (d) If the Commission's report is submitted under subparagraph (c), the States Parties concerned shall, within three months of the receipt of the report, notify the Chairman of the Committee whether or not they accept the contents of the report of the Commission.

8. The provisions of this article are without prejudice to the responsibilities of the Committee under article 41.

9. The States Parties concerned shall share equally all the expenses of the members of the Commission in accordance with estimates to be provided by the Secretary-General of the United Nations.

10. The Secretary-General of the United Nations shall be empowered to pay the expenses of the members of the Commission, if necessary, before reimbursement by the States Parties concerned, in accordance with paragraph 9 of this article.

Article 43

The members of the Committee, and of the ad hoc conciliation commissions which may be appointed under article 42, shall be entitled to the facilities, privileges and immunities of experts on mission for the United Nations as laid down in the relevant sections of the Convention on the Privileges and Immunities of the United Nations.

Article 44

The provisions for the implementation of the present Covenant shall apply without prejudice to the procedures prescribed in the field of human rights by or under the constituent instruments and the conventions of the United Nations and of the specialized agencies and shall not prevent the States Parties to the present Covenant from having recourse to other procedures for settling a dispute in accordance with general or special international agreements in force between them.

Article 45

The Committee shall submit to the General Assembly of the United Nations, through the Economic and Social Council, an annual report on its activities.

PART V

Article 46

Nothing in the present Covenant shall be interpreted as impairing the provisions of the Charter of the United Nations and of the constitutions of the specialized agencies which define the respective responsibilities of the various organs of the United Nations and of the specialized agencies in regard to the matters dealt with in the present Covenant.

Article 47

Nothing in the present Covenant shall be interpreted as impairing the inherent right of all peoples to enjoy and utilize fully and freely their natural wealth and resources.

PART VI

Article 48

1. The present Covenant is open for signature by any State Member of the United Nations or member of any of its specialized agencies, by any State Party to the Statute of the International Court of Justice, and by any other State which has been invited by the General Assembly of the United Nations to become a Party to the present Covenant.

2. The present Covenant is subject to ratification. Instruments of ratification shall be deposited with the Secretary-General of the United Nations.

3. The present Covenant shall be open to accession by any State referred to in paragraph 1 of this article.

4. Accession shall be effected by the deposit of an instrument of accession with the Secretary-General of the United Nations.

5. The Secretary-General of the United Nations shall inform all States which have signed this Covenant or acceded to it of the deposit of each instrument of ratification or accession.

Article 49

1. The present Covenant shall enter into force three months after the date of the deposit with the Secretary-General of the United Nations of the thirty-fifth instrument of ratification or instrument of accession.

2. For each State ratifying the present Covenant or acceding to it after the deposit of the thirty-fifth instrument of ratification or instrument of accession, the present Covenant shall enter into force three months after the date of the deposit of its own instrument of ratification or instrument of accession.

Article 50

The provisions of the present Covenant shall extend to all parts of federal States without any limitations or exceptions.

Article 51

1. Any State Party to the present Covenant may propose an amendment and file it with the Secretary-General of the United Nations. The Secretary-General of the United Nations shall thereupon communicate any proposed amendments to the

States Parties to the present Covenant with a request that they notify him whether they favour a conference of States Parties for the purpose of considering and voting upon the proposals. In the event that at least one third of the States Parties favours such a conference, the Secretary-General shall convene the conference under the auspices of the United Nations. Any amendment adopted by a majority of the States Parties present and voting at the conference shall be submitted to the General Assembly of the United Nations for approval.

2. Amendments shall come into force when they have been approved by the General Assembly of the United Nations and accepted by a two-thirds majority of the States Parties to the present Covenant in accordance with their respective constitutional processes.

3. When amendments come into force, they shall be binding on those States Parties which have accepted them, other States Parties still being bound by the provisions of the present Covenant and any earlier amendment which they have accepted.

Article 52

Irrespective of the notifications made under article 48, paragraph 5, the Secretary-General of the United Nations shall inform all States referred to in paragraph I of the same article of the following particulars:

(a) Signatures, ratifications and accessions under article 48;

(b) The date of the entry into force of the present Covenant under article 49 and the date of the entry into force of any amendments under article 51.

Article 53

1. The present Covenant, of which the Chinese, English, French, Russian and Spanish texts are equally authentic, shall be deposited in the archives of the United Nations.

2. The Secretary-General of the United Nations shall transmit certified copies of the present Covenant to all States referred to in article 48.

APPENDIX IV
Economic and Social Council Resolution 1985/ 17 on the Committee on Economic, Social and Cultural Rights

1985/ 17. Review of the composition, organization and administrative arrangements of the Sessional Working Group of Governmental Experts on the Implementation of the International Covenant on Economic, Social and Cultural Rights

The Economic and Social Council,

Recalling its resolution 1988 (LX) of 11 May 1976, by which it noted the important responsibilities placed upon the Economic and Social Council by the International Covenant on Economic, Social and Cultural Rights,[1] in particular those resulting from articles 21 and 22 of the Covenant, and expressed its readiness to fulfil those responsibilities,

Recalling its decision 1978/10 of 3 May 1978, by which it decided to establish a Sessional Working Group on the Implementation of the International Covenant on Economic, Social and Cultural Rights, for the purpose of assisting the Council in the consideration of reports submitted by States parties to the Covenant in accordance with Council resolution 1988 (LX), and determined the composition of the Working Group,

Recalling also its resolution 1979/43 of 11 May 1979, by which it approved the methods of work of the Working Group, and its decision 1981/158 of 8 May 1981, by which it incorporated certain changes in, and modified the methods of work of, the Working Group,

Recalling further its resolution 1982/33 of 6 May 1982, by which it modified the composition, organization and administrative arrangements of the Sessional Working Group of Governmental Experts and decided to review the composition, organization and administrative arrangements of the Group at its first regular session of 1985,

---

[1] General Assembly resolution 2200 (XXI).

Having considered the report of the Secretary-General on the composition, organization and administrative arrangements of the Sessional Working Group of Governmental Experts on the Implementation of the International Covenant on Economic, Social and Cultural Rights and other bodies established in accordance with existing international instruments in the field of human rights,[2]

Having considered the report of the Sessional Working Group of Governmental Experts on the Implementation of the International Covenant on Economic, Social and Cultural Rights,[3]

Decides that:

(a) The Working Group established by Economic and Social Council decision 1978/10 and modified by Council decision 1981/158 and resolution 1982/33 shall be renamed "Committee on Economic, Social and Cultural Rights" (hereinafter referred to as "the Committee");

(b) The Committee shall have eighteen members who shall be experts with recognized competence in the field of human rights, serving in their personal capacity, due consideration being given to equitable geographical distribution and to the representation of different forms of social and legal systems; to this end, fifteen seats will be equally distributed among the regional groups, while the additional three seats will be allocated in accordance with the increase in the total number of States parties per regional group;

(c) The members of the Committee shall be elected by the Council by secret ballot from a list of persons nominated by States parties to the International Covenant on Economic, Social and Cultural Rights under the following conditions:

(i) The members of the Committee shall be elected for a term of four years and shall be eligible for re-election at the end of their term, if renominated;

(ii) One half of the membership of the Committee shall be renewed every second year, bearing in mind the need to maintain the equitable geographical distribution mentioned in subparagraph *(b)* above;

(iii) The first elections shall take place during the Council's first regular session of 1986; immediately after the first elections, the President of the

---

[2] E/1985/17.
[3] E/1985/18.

Council shall choose by lot the names of nine members whose term shall expire at the end of two years;

(iv) The terms of office of members elected to the Committee shall begin on 1 January following their election and expire on 31 December following the election of members that are to succeed them as members of the Committee;

(v) Subsequent elections shall take place every second year during the first regular session of the Council;

(vi) At least four months before the date of each election to the Committee the Secretary-General shall address a written invitation to the States parties to the Covenant to submit their nominations for membership of the Committee within three months; the Secretary-General shall prepare a list of the persons thus nominated, with an indication of the States parties which have nominated them, and shall submit it to the Council no later than one month before the date of each election;

(d) The Committee shall meet annually for a period of up to three weeks, taking into account the number of reports to be examined by the Committee, with the venue alternating between Geneva and New York;

(e) The members of the Committee shall receive travel and subsistence expenses from United Nations resources;

(f) The Committee shall submit to the Council a report on its activities, including a summary of its consideration of the reports submitted by a States parties to the Covenant, and shall make suggestions and recommendations of a general nature on the basis of its consideration of those reports and of the reports submitted by the specialized agencies, in order to assist the Council to fulfil, in particular, its responsibilities under articles 21 and 22 of the Covenant;

(g) The Secretary-General shall provide the Committee with summary records of its proceedings, which shall be made available to the Council at the same time as the report of the Committee; the Secretary-General shall further provide the Committee with the necessary staff and facilities for the effective performance of its functions, bearing in mind the need to give adequate publicity to its work;

(h) The procedures and methods of work established by Council resolution 1979/43 and the other resolutions and decisions referred to in the preamble to the present resolution shall remain in force in so far as they are not superseded or modified by the present resolution;

(i) The Council shall review the composition, organization and administrative arrangements of the Committee at its first regular session of 1990, and subsequently every five years, taking into account the principle of equitable geographical distribution of its membership.

22nd plenary meeting

28 May 1985

APPENDIX V
General Comment No. 15—The Right to Water

Committee on Economic, Social and Cultural Rights
Twenty-ninth session
Geneva, 11–29 November 2002
Agenda item 3

Substantive Issues Arising in the Implementation of the International Covenant on Economic, Social and Cultural Rights

General Comment No. 15 (2002)

The right to water (arts. 11 and 12 of the International Covenant on Economic, Social and Cultural Rights)

I. INTRODUCTION

1. Water is a limited natural resource and a public good fundamental for life and health. The human right to water is indispensable for leading a life in human dignity. It is a prerequisite for the realization of other human rights. The Committee has been confronted continually with the widespread denial of the right to water in developing as well as developed countries. Over one billion persons lack access to a basic water supply, while several billions do not have access to adequate sanitation, which is the primary cause of water contamination and diseases linked to water.[1] The continuing contamination, depletion and unequal

---

[1] In 2000, the World Health Organization estimated that 1.1 billion persons did not have access to an improved water supply (80 per cent of them rural dwellers) able to provide at least 20 litres of safe water per person a day; 2.4 billion persons were estimated to be without sanitation. (See WHO, *The Global Water Supply and Sanitation Assessment 2000,* Geneva, 2000, p.1.) Further, 2.3 billion persons each year suffer from diseases linked to water: see United Nations, Commission on Sustainable Development, *Comprehensive Assessment of the Freshwater Resources of the World*, New York, 1997, p. 39.

distribution of water is exacerbating existing poverty. States parties have to adopt effective measures to realize, without discrimination, the right to water, as set out in this general comment.

The legal bases of the right to water

2. The human right to water entitles everyone to sufficient, safe, acceptable, physically accessible and affordable water for personal and domestic uses. An adequate amount of safe water is necessary to prevent death from dehydration, to reduce the risk of water-related disease and to provide for consumption, cooking, personal and domestic hygienic requirements.

3. Article 11, paragraph 1, of the Covenant specifies a number of rights emanating from, and indispensable for, the realization of the right to an adequate standard of living "including adequate food, clothing and housing." The use of the word "including" indicates that this catalogue of rights was not intended to be exhaustive. The right to water clearly falls within the category of guarantees essential for securing an adequate standard of living, particularly since it is one of the most fundamental conditions for survival. Moreover, the Committee has previously recognized that water is a human right contained in article 11, paragraph 1, (see General Comment No. 6 (1995)).[2] The right to water is also inextricably related to the right to the highest attainable standard of health (art. 12, para. 1)[3] and the rights to adequate housing and adequate food (art. 11, para. 1).[4] The right should also be seen in conjunction with other rights enshrined in the International Bill of Human Rights, foremost amongst them the right to life and human dignity.

4. The right to water has been recognized in a wide range of international documents, including treaties, declarations and other standards.[5] For instance, Article

---

[2] See paras. 5 and 32 of the Committee's General Comment No. 6 (1995) on the economic, social and cultural rights of older persons.

[3] See General Comment No. 14 (2000) on the right to the highest attainable standard of health, paragraphs 11, 12 (*a*), (*b*) and (*d*), 15, 34, 36, 40, 43 and 51.

[4] See para. 8 (*b*) of General Comment No. 4 (1991). See also the report by Commission on Human Rights' Special Rapporteur on adequate housing as a component of the right to an adequate standard of living, Mr. Miloon Kothari (E.CN.4/2002/59), submitted in accordance with Commission resolution 2001/28 of 20 April 2001. In relation to the right to adequate food, see the report by the Special Rapporteur of the Commission on the right to food, Mr. Jean Ziegler (E/CN.4/2002/58), submitted in accordance with Commission resolution 2001/25 of 20 April 2001.

[5] See art. 14, para. 2 (*h*), Convention on the Elimination of All Forms of Discrimination against Women; art. 24, para. 2 (*c*), Convention on the Rights of the Child; arts. 20, 26, 29 and 46 of the

14, paragraph 2, of the Convention on the Elimination of All Forms of Discrimination against Women stipulates that States parties shall ensure to women the right to "enjoy adequate living conditions, particularly in relation to [. . .] water supply." Article 24, paragraph 2, of the Convention on the Rights of the Child requires States parties to combat disease and malnutrition "through the provision of adequate nutritious foods and clean drinking-water."

5. The right to water has been consistently addressed by the Committee during its consideration of States parties' reports, in accordance with its revised general guidelines regarding the form and content of reports to be submitted by States parties under articles 16 and 17 of the International Covenant on Economic, Social and Cultural Rights, and its general comments.

6. Water is required for a range of different purposes, besides personal and domestic uses, to realize many of the Covenant rights. For instance, water is necessary to produce food (right to adequate food) and ensure environmental hygiene (right to health). Water is essential for securing livelihoods (right to gain a living by work) and enjoying certain cultural practices (right to take part in cultural life). Nevertheless, priority in the allocation of water must be given to the right to water for personal and domestic uses. Priority should also be given to the water resources required to prevent starvation and disease, as well as water required to meet the core obligations of each of the Covenant rights.[6]

Geneva Convention relative to the Treatment of Prisoners of War, of 1949; arts. 85, 89 and 127 of the Geneva Convention relative to the Treatment of Civilian Persons in Time of War, of 1949; arts. 54 and 55 of Additional Protocol I thereto of 1977; arts. 5 and 14 Additional Protocol II of 1977; preamble, Mar Del Plata Action Plan of the United Nations Water Conference; see para. 18.47 of Agenda 21, *Report of the United Nations Conference on Environment and Development, Rio de Janeiro, 3-14 June 1992* (A/CONF.151/26/Rev.1 (Vol. I and Vol. I/Corr.1, Vol. II, Vol. III and Vol. III/Corr.1) (United Nations publication, Sales No. E.93.I.8), vol. I: *Resolutions adopted by the Conference*, resolution 1, annex II; Principle No. 3, The Dublin Statement on Water and Sustainable Development, International Conference on Water and the Environment (A/CONF.151/PC/112); Principle No. 2, Programme of Action, *Report of the United Nations International Conference on Population and Development, Cairo, 5-13 September 1994* (United Nations publication, Sales No. E.95.XIII.18), chap. I, resolution 1, annex; paras. 5 and 19, Recommendation (2001) 14 of the Committee of Ministers to Member States on the European Charter on Water Resources; resolution 2002/6 of the United Nations Sub-Commission on the Promotion and Protection of Human Rights on the promotion of the realization of the right to drinking water. See also the report on the relationship between the enjoyment of economic, social and cultural rights and the promotion of the realization of the right to drinking water supply and sanitation (E/CN.4/Sub.2/2002/10) submitted by the Special Rapporteur of the Sub-Commission on the right to drinking water supply and sanitation, Mr. El Hadji Guissé.

[6] See also World Summit on Sustainable Development, Plan of Implementation 2002, paragraph 25 (*c*).

Water and Covenant rights

7. The Committee notes the importance of ensuring sustainable access to water resources for agriculture to realize the right to adequate food (see General Comment No.12 (1999)).[7] Attention should be given to ensuring that disadvantaged and marginalized farmers, including women farmers, have equitable access to water and water management systems, including sustainable rain harvesting and irrigation technology. Taking note of the duty in article 1, paragraph 2, of the Covenant, which provides that a people may not "be deprived of its means of subsistence," States parties should ensure that there is adequate access to water for subsistence farming and for securing the livelihoods of indigenous peoples.[8]

8. Environmental hygiene, as an aspect of the right to health under article 12, paragraph 2 *(b)*, of the Covenant, encompasses taking steps on a non-discriminatory basis to prevent threats to health from unsafe and toxic water conditions.[9] For example, States parties should ensure that natural water resources are protected from contamination by harmful substances and pathogenic microbes. Likewise, States parties should monitor and combat situations where aquatic eco-systems serve as a habitat for vectors of diseases wherever they pose a risk to human living environments.[10]

9. With a view to assisting States parties' implementation of the Covenant and the fulfilment of their reporting obligations, this General Comment focuses in Part II on the normative content of the right to water in articles 11, paragraph 1, and 12, on States parties' obligations (Part III), on violations (Part IV) and on implementation at the national level (Part V), while the obligations of actors other than States parties are addressed in Part VI.

---

[7] This relates to both *availability* and to *accessibility* of the right to adequate food (see General Comment No. 12 (1999), paras. 12 and 13).

[8] See also the Statement of Understanding accompanying the United Nations Convention on the Law of Non-Navigational Uses of Watercourses (A/51/869 of 11 April 1997), which declared that, in determining vital human needs in the event of conflicts over the use of watercourses "special attention is to be paid to providing sufficient water to sustain human life, including both drinking water and water required for production of food in order to prevent starvation."

[9] See also para. 15, General Comment No. 14.

[10] According to the WHO definition, vector-borne diseases include diseases transmitted by insects (malaria, filariasis, dengue, Japanese encephalitis and yellow fever), diseases for which aquatic snails serve as intermediate hosts (schistosomiasis) and zoonoses with vertebrates as reservoir hosts.

II. NORMATIVE CONTENT OF THE RIGHT TO WATER

10. The right to water contains both freedoms and entitlements. The freedoms include the right to maintain access to existing water supplies necessary for the right to water, and the right to be free from interference, such as the right to be free from arbitrary disconnections or contamination of water supplies. By contrast, the entitlements include the right to a system of water supply and management that provides equality of opportunity for people to enjoy the right to water.

11. The elements of the right to water must be *adequate* for human dignity, life and health, in accordance with articles 11, paragraph 1, and 12. The adequacy of water should not be interpreted narrowly, by mere reference to volumetric quantities and technologies. Water should be treated as a social and cultural good, and not primarily as an economic good. The manner of the realization of the right to water must also be sustainable, ensuring that the right can be realized for present and future generations.[11]

12. While the adequacy of water required for the right to water may vary according to different conditions, the following factors apply in all circumstances:

(a) *Availability*. The water supply for each person must be sufficient and continuous for personal and domestic uses.[12] These uses ordinarily include drinking, personal sanitation, washing of clothes, food preparation, personal and household hygiene.[13] The quantity of water available for each person should correspond to World Health Organization (WHO) guidelines.[14] Some

---

[11] For a definition of sustainability, see the *Report of the United Nations Conference on Environment and Development, Rio de Janeiro, 3-14 [June] 1992*, Declaration on Environment and Development, principles 1, 8, 9, 10, 12 and 15; and Agenda 21, in particular principles 5.3, 7.27, 7.28, 7.35, 7.39, 7.41, 18.3, 18.8, 18.35, 18.40, 18.48, 18.50, 18.59 and 18.68.

[12] "Continuous" means that the regularity of the water supply is sufficient for personal and domestic uses.

[13] In this context, "drinking" means water for consumption through beverages and foodstuffs. "Personal sanitation" means disposal of human excreta. Water is necessary for personal sanitation where water-based means are adopted. "Food preparation" includes food hygiene and preparation of food stuffs, whether water is incorporated into, or comes into contact with, food. "Personal and household hygiene" means personal cleanliness and hygiene of the household environment.

[14] See J. Bartram and G. Howard, "Domestic water quantity, service level and health: what should be the goal for water and health sectors," WHO, 2002. See also P. H. Gleick, (1996) "Basic water requirements for human activities: meeting basic needs," *Water International*, 21, pp. 83-92.

individuals and groups may also require additional water due to health, climate, and work conditions;

(b) *Quality*. The water required for each personal or domestic use must be safe, therefore free from micro-organisms, chemical substances and radiological *hazards* that constitute a threat to a person's health.[15] Furthermore, water should be of an acceptable colour, odour and taste for each personal or domestic use.

(c) *Accessibility*. Water and water facilities and services have to be accessible to *everyone* without discrimination, within the jurisdiction of the State party. Accessibility has four overlapping dimensions:

(i) *Physical accessibility*: water, and adequate water facilities and services, must be within safe physical reach for all sections of the population. Sufficient, safe and acceptable water must be accessible within, or in the immediate vicinity, of each household, educational institution and workplace.[16] All water facilities and services must be of sufficient quality, culturally appropriate and sensitive to gender, life-cycle and privacy requirements. Physical security should not be threatened during access to water facilities and services;

(ii) *Economic accessibility*: Water, and water facilities and services, must be affordable for all. The direct and indirect costs and charges associated with securing water must be affordable, and must not compromise or threaten the realization of other Covenant rights;

(iii) *Non-discrimination*: Water and water facilities and services must be accessible to all, including the most vulnerable or marginalized sections of the population, in law and in fact, without discrimination on any of the prohibited grounds; and

(iv) *Information accessibility*: accessibility includes the right to seek, receive and impart information concerning water issues.[17]

---

[15] The Committee refers States parties to WHO, *Guidelines for drinking-water quality,* 2nd edition, vols. 1-3 (Geneva, 1993) that are "intended to be used as a basis for the development of national standards that, if properly implemented, will ensure the safety of drinking water supplies through the elimination of, or reduction to a minimum concentration, of constituents of water that are known to be hazardous to health."

[16] See also General Comment No. 4 (1991), para. 8 (*b*), General Comment No. 13 (1999) para. 6 (*a*) and General Comment No. 14 (2000) paras. 8 (*a*) and (b). Household includes a permanent or semi-permanent dwelling, or a temporary halting site.

[17] See para. 48 of this General Comment.

Special topics of broad application

Non-discrimination and equality

13. The obligation of States parties to guarantee that the right to water is enjoyed without discrimination (art. 2, para. 2), and equally between men and women (art. 3), pervades all of the Covenant obligations. The Covenant thus proscribes any discrimination on the grounds of race, colour, sex, age, language, religion, political or other opinion, national or social origin, property, birth, physical or mental disability, health status (including HIV/AIDS), sexual orientation and civil, political, social or other status, which has the intention or effect of nullifying or impairing the equal enjoyment or exercise of the right to water. The Committee recalls paragraph 12 of General Comment No. 3 (1990), which states that even in times of severe resource constraints, the vulnerable members of society must be protected by the adoption of relatively low-cost targeted programmes.

14. States parties should take steps to remove de facto discrimination on prohibited grounds, where individuals and groups are deprived of the means or entitlements necessary for achieving the right to water. States parties should ensure that the allocation of water resources, and investments in water, facilitate access to water for all members of society. Inappropriate resource allocation can lead to discrimination that may not be overt. For example, investments should not disproportionately favour expensive water supply services and facilities that are often accessible only to a small, privileged fraction of the population, rather than investing in services and facilities that benefit a far larger part of the population.

15. With respect to the right to water, States parties have a special obligation to provide those who do not have sufficient means with the necessary water and water facilities and to prevent any discrimination on internationally prohibited grounds in the provision of water and water services.

16. Whereas the right to water applies to everyone, States parties should give special attention to those individuals and groups who have traditionally faced difficulties in exercising this right, including women, children, minority groups, indigenous peoples, refugees, asylum seekers, internally displaced persons, migrant workers, prisoners and detainees. In particular, States parties should take steps to ensure that:

(a) Women are not excluded from decision-making processes concerning water resources and entitlements. The disproportionate burden women bear in the collection of water should be alleviated;

(b) Children are not prevented from enjoying their human rights due to the lack of adequate water in educational institutions and households or through the burden of collecting water. Provision of adequate water to educational institutions currently without adequate drinking water should be addressed as a matter of urgency;

(c) Rural and deprived urban areas have access to properly maintained water facilities. Access to traditional water sources in rural areas should be protected from unlawful encroachment and pollution. Deprived urban areas, including informal human settlements, and homeless persons, should have access to properly maintained water facilities. No household should be denied the right to water on the grounds of their housing or land status;

(d) Indigenous peoples' access to water resources on their ancestral lands is protected from encroachment and unlawful pollution. States should provide resources for indigenous peoples to design, deliver and control their access to water;

(e) Nomadic and traveller communities have access to adequate water at traditional and designated halting sites;

(f) Refugees, asylum-seekers, internally displaced persons and returnees have access to adequate water whether they stay in camps or in urban and rural areas. Refugees and asylum-seekers should be granted the right to water on the same conditions as granted to nationals;

(g) Prisoners and detainees are provided with sufficient and safe water for their daily individual requirements, taking note of the requirements of international humanitarian law and the United Nations Standard Minimum Rules for the Treatment of Prisoners;[18]

(h) Groups facing difficulties with physical access to water, such as older persons, persons with disabilities, victims of natural disasters, persons living in disaster-prone areas, and those living in arid and semi-arid areas, or on small islands are provided with safe and sufficient water.

---

[18] See arts. 20, 26, 29 and 46 of the third Geneva Convention of 12 August 1949; arts. 85, 89 and 127 of the fourth Geneva Convention of 12 August 1949; arts. 15 and 20, para. 2, United Nations Standard Minimum Rules for the Treatment of Prisoners, in *Human Rights: A Compilation of International Instruments* (United Nations publication, Sales No. E.88.XIV.1).

III. STATES PARTIES' OBLIGATIONS

General legal obligations

17. While the Covenant provides for progressive realization and acknowledges the constraints due to the limits of available resources, it also imposes on States parties various obligations which are of immediate effect. States parties have immediate obligations in relation to the right to water, such as the guarantee that the right will be exercised without discrimination of any kind (art. 2, para. 2) and the obligation to take steps (art. 2, para.1) towards the full realization of articles 11, paragraph 1, and 12. Such steps must be deliberate, concrete and targeted towards the full realization of the right to water.

18. States parties have a constant and continuing duty under the Covenant to move as expeditiously and effectively as possible towards the full realization of the right to water. Realization of the right should be feasible and practicable, since all States parties exercise control over a broad range of resources, including water, technology, financial resources and international assistance, as with all other rights in the Covenant.

19. There is a strong presumption that retrogressive measures taken in relation to the right to water are prohibited under the Covenant.[19] If any deliberately retrogressive measures are taken, the State party has the burden of proving that they have been introduced after the most careful consideration of all alternatives and that they are duly justified by reference to the totality of the rights provided for in the Covenant in the context of the full use of the State party's maximum available resources.

Specific legal obligations

20. The right to water, like any human right, imposes three types of obligations on States parties: obligations to *respect*, obligations to *protect* and obligations to *fulfil*.

(a) Obligations to respect

21. The obligation to *respect* requires that States parties refrain from interfering directly or indirectly with the enjoyment of the right to water. The obligation

---

[19] See General Comment No. 3 (1990), para. 9.

includes, inter alia, refraining from engaging in any practice or activity that denies or limits equal access to adequate water; arbitrarily interfering with customary or traditional arrangements for water allocation; unlawfully diminishing or polluting water, for example through waste from State-owned facilities or through use and testing of weapons; and limiting access to, or destroying, water services and infrastructure as a punitive measure, for example, during armed conflicts in violation of international humanitarian law.

22. The Committee notes that during armed conflicts, emergency situations and natural disasters, the right to water embraces those obligations by which States parties are bound under international humanitarian law.[20] This includes protection of objects indispensable for survival of the civilian population, including drinking water installations and supplies and irrigation works, protection of the natural environment against widespread, long-term and severe damage and ensuring that civilians, internees and prisoners have access to adequate water.[21]

(b) Obligations to protect

23. The obligation to *protect* requires State parties to prevent third parties from interfering in any way with the enjoyment of the right to water. Third parties include individuals, groups, corporations and other entities as well as agents acting under their authority. The obligation includes, inter alia, adopting the necessary and effective legislative and other measures to restrain, for example, third parties from denying equal access to adequate water; and polluting and inequitably extracting from water resources, including natural sources, wells and other water distribution systems.

24. Where water services (such as piped water networks, water tankers, access to rivers and wells) are operated or controlled by third parties, States parties must prevent them from compromising equal, affordable, and physical access to sufficient, safe and acceptable water. To prevent such abuses an effective regulatory system must be established, in conformity with the Covenant and this General Comment, which includes independent monitoring, genuine public participation and imposition of penalties for non-compliance.

---

[20] For the interrelationship of human rights law and humanitarian law, the Committee notes the conclusions of the International Court of Justice in *Legality of the Threat or Use of Nuclear Weapons (Request by the General Assembly), ICJ Reports (1996)* p. 226, para. 25.

[21] See arts. 54 and 56, Additional Protocol I to the Geneva Conventions (1977), art. 54, Additional Protocol II (1977), arts. 20 and 46 of the third Geneva Convention of 12 August 1949, and common article 3 of the Geneva Conventions of 12 August 1949.

(c) Obligations to fulfil

25. The obligation to *fulfil* can be disaggregated into the obligations to facilitate, promote and provide. The obligation to facilitate requires the State to take positive measures to assist individuals and communities to enjoy the right. The obligation to promote obliges the State party to take steps to ensure that there is appropriate education concerning the hygienic use of water, protection of water sources and methods to minimize water wastage. States parties are also obliged to fulfil (provide) the right when individuals or a group are unable, for reasons beyond their control, to realize that right themselves by the means at their disposal.

26. The obligation to fulfil requires States parties to adopt the necessary measures directed towards the full realization of the right to water. The obligation includes, inter alia, according sufficient recognition of this right within the national political and legal systems, preferably by way of legislative implementation; adopting a national water strategy and plan of action to realize this right; ensuring that water is affordable for everyone; and facilitating improved and sustainable access to water, particularly in rural and deprived urban areas.

27. To ensure that water is affordable, States parties must adopt the necessary measures that may include, inter alia: *(a)* use of a range of appropriate low-cost techniques and technologies; *(b)* appropriate pricing policies such as free or low-cost water; and *(c)* income supplements. Any payment for water services has to be based on the principle of equity, ensuring that these services, whether privately or publicly provided, are affordable for all, including socially disadvantaged groups. Equity demands that poorer households should not be disproportionately burdened with water expenses as compared to richer households.

28. States parties should adopt comprehensive and integrated strategies and programmes to ensure that there is sufficient and safe water for present and future generations.[22] Such strategies and programmes may include: *(a)* reducing depletion of water resources through unsustainable extraction, diversion and damming; *(b)* reducing and eliminating contamination of watersheds and water-related ecosystems by substances such as radiation, harmful chemicals and human excreta; *(c)* monitoring water reserves; *(d)* ensuring that proposed developments do not interfere with access to adequate water; *(e)* assessing the impacts of actions that

---

[22] See footnote 5 above, Agenda 21, chaps. 5, 7 and 18; and the World Summit on Sustainable Development, Plan of Implementation (2002), paras. 6 (*a*), (*l*) and (*m*), 7, 36 and 38.

may impinge upon water availability and natural-ecosystems watersheds, such as climate changes, desertification and increased soil salinity, deforestation and loss of biodiversity;[23] *(f)* increasing the efficient use of water by end-users; *(g)* reducing water wastage in its distribution; *(h)* response mechanisms for emergency situations; and *(i)* establishing competent institutions and appropriate institutional arrangements to carry out the strategies and programmes.

29. Ensuring that everyone has access to adequate sanitation is not only fundamental for human dignity and privacy, but is one of the principal mechanisms for protecting the quality of drinking water supplies and resources.[24] In accordance with the rights to health and adequate housing (see General Comments No. 4 (1991) and 14 (2000)) States parties have an obligation to progressively extend safe sanitation services, particularly to rural and deprived urban areas, taking into account the needs of women and children.

International obligations

30. Article 2, paragraph 1, and articles 11, paragraph 1, and 23 of the Covenant require that States parties recognize the essential role of international cooperation and assistance and take joint and separate action to achieve the full realization of the right to water.

31. To comply with their international obligations in relation to the right to water, States parties have to respect the enjoyment of the right in other countries. International cooperation requires States parties to refrain from actions that interfere, directly or indirectly, with the enjoyment of the right to water in other countries. Any activities undertaken within the State party's jurisdiction should not deprive another country of the ability to realize the right to water for persons in its jurisdiction.[25]

---

[23] See the Convention on Biological Diversity, the Convention to Combat Desertification, the United Nations Framework Convention on Climate Change, and subsequent protocols.

[24] Article 14, para. 2, of the Convention on the Elimination of All Forms of Discrimination against Women stipulates States parties shall ensure to women the right to "adequate living conditions, particularly in relation to [. . .] sanitation." Article 24, para. 2, of the Convention on the Rights of the Child requires States parties to "To ensure that all segments of society [. . .] have access to education and are supported in the use of basic knowledge of [. . .] the advantages of [. . .] hygiene and environmental sanitation."

[25] The Committee notes that the United Nations Convention on the Law of Non-Navigational Uses of Watercourses requires that social and human needs be taken into account in determining the equitable utilization of watercourses, that States parties take measures to prevent

32. States parties should refrain at all times from imposing embargoes or similar measures, that prevent the supply of water, as well as goods and services essential for securing the right to water.[26] Water should never be used as an instrument of political and economic pressure. In this regard, the Committee recalls its position, stated in its General Comment No. 8 (1997), on the relationship between economic sanctions and respect for economic, social and cultural rights.

33. Steps should be taken by States parties to prevent their own citizens and companies from violating the right to water of individuals and communities in other countries. Where States parties can take steps to influence other third parties to respect the right, through legal or political means, such steps should be taken in accordance with the Charter of the United Nations and applicable international law.

34. Depending on the availability of resources, States should facilitate realization of the right to water in other countries, for example through provision of water resources, financial and technical assistance, and provide the necessary aid when required. In disaster relief and emergency assistance, including assistance to refugees and displaced persons, priority should be given to Covenant rights, including the provision of adequate water. International assistance should be provided in a manner that is consistent with the Covenant and other human rights standards, and sustainable and culturally appropriate. The economically developed States parties have a special responsibility and interest to assist the poorer developing States in this regard.

35. States parties should ensure that the right to water is given due attention in international agreements and, to that end, should consider the development of further legal instruments. With regard to the conclusion and implementation of other international and regional agreements, States parties should take steps to ensure that these instruments do not adversely impact upon the right to water. Agreements concerning trade liberalization should not curtail or inhibit a country's capacity to ensure the full realization of the right to water.

---

significant harm being caused, and, in the event of conflict, special regard must be given to the requirements of vital human needs: see arts. 5, 7 and 10 of the Convention.

[26] In General Comment No. 8 (1997), the Committee noted the disruptive effect of sanctions upon sanitation supplies and clean drinking water, and that sanctions regimes should provide for repairs to infrastructure essential to provide clean water.

36. States parties should ensure that their actions as members of international organizations take due account of the right to water. Accordingly, States parties that are members of international financial institutions, notably the International Monetary Fund, the World Bank, and regional development banks, should take steps to ensure that the right to water is taken into account in their lending policies, credit agreements and other international measures.

Core obligations

37. In General Comment No. 3 (1990), the Committee confirms that States parties have a core obligation to ensure the satisfaction of, at the very least, minimum essential levels of each of the rights enunciated in the Covenant. In the Committee's view, at least a number of core obligations in relation to the right to water can be identified, which are of immediate effect:

(a) To ensure access to the minimum essential amount of water, that is sufficient and safe for personal and domestic uses to prevent disease;

(b) To ensure the right of access to water and water facilities and services on a non-discriminatory basis, especially for disadvantaged or marginalized groups;

(c) To ensure physical access to water facilities or services that provide sufficient, safe and regular water; that have a sufficient number of water outlets to avoid prohibitive waiting times; and that are at a reasonable distance from the household;

(d) To ensure personal security is not threatened when having to physically access to water;

(e) To ensure equitable distribution of all available water facilities and services;

(f) To adopt and implement a national water strategy and plan of action addressing the whole population; the strategy and plan of action should be devised, and periodically reviewed, on the basis of a participatory and transparent process; it should include methods, such as right to water indicators and benchmarks, by which progress can be closely monitored; the process by which the strategy and plan of action are devised, as well as their content, shall give particular attention to all disadvantaged or marginalized groups;

(g) To monitor the extent of the realization, or the non-realization, of the right to water;

(h) To adopt relatively low-cost targeted water programmes to protect vulnerable and marginalized groups;

(i) To take measures to prevent, treat and control diseases linked to water, in particular ensuring access to adequate sanitation;

38. For the avoidance of any doubt, the Committee wishes to emphasize that it is particularly incumbent on States parties, and other actors in a position to assist, to provide international assistance and cooperation, especially economic and technical which enables developing countries to fulfil their core obligations indicated in paragraph 37 above.

IV. VIOLATIONS

39. When the normative content of the right to water (see Part II) is applied to the obligations of States parties (Part III), a process is set in motion, which facilitates identification of violations of the right to water. The following paragraphs provide illustrations of violations of the right to water.

40. To demonstrate compliance with their general and specific obligations, States parties must establish that they have taken the necessary and feasible steps towards the realization of the right to water. In accordance with international law, a failure to act in good faith to take such steps amounts to a violation of the right. It should be stressed that a State party cannot justify its non-compliance with the core obligations set out in paragraph 37 above, which are non-derogable.

41. In determining which actions or omissions amount to a violation of the right to water, it is important to distinguish the inability from the unwillingness of a State party to comply with its obligations in relation to the right to water. This follows from articles 11, paragraph 1, and 12, which speak of the right to an adequate standard of living and the right to health, as well as from article 2, paragraph 1, of the Covenant, which obliges each State party to take the necessary steps to the maximum of its available resources. A State which is unwilling to use the maximum of its available resources for the realization of the right to water is in violation of its obligations under the Covenant. If resource constraints render it impossible for a State party to comply fully with its Covenant obligations, it has the burden of justifying that every effort has nevertheless been made to use all available resources at its disposal in order to satisfy, as a matter of priority, the obligations outlined above.

42. Violations of the right to water can occur through acts of *commission*, the direct actions of States parties or other entities insufficiently regulated by States. Violations include, for example, the adoption of retrogressive measures incompatible with the core obligations (outlined in para. 37 above), the formal repeal or suspension of legislation necessary for the continued enjoyment of the right to water, or the adoption of legislation or policies which are manifestly incompatible with pre-existing domestic or international legal obligations in relation to the right to water.

43. Violations through *acts of omission* include the failure to take appropriate steps towards the full realization of everyone's right to water, the failure to have a national policy on water, and the failure to enforce relevant laws.

44. While it is not possible to specify a complete list of violations in advance, a number of typical examples relating to the levels of obligations, emanating from the Committee's work, may be identified:

(a) Violations of the obligation to respect follow from the State party's interference with the right to water. This includes, inter alia: *(i)* arbitrary or unjustified disconnection or exclusion from water services or facilities; *(ii)* discriminatory or unaffordable increases in the price of water; and *(iii)* pollution and diminution of water resources affecting human health;

(b) Violations of the obligation to protect follow from the failure of a State to take all necessary measures to safeguard persons within their jurisdiction from infringements of the right to water by third parties.[27] This includes, inter alia: *(i)* failure to enact or enforce laws to prevent the contamination and inequitable extraction of water; *(ii)* failure to effectively regulate and control water services providers; *(iii)* failure to protect water distribution systems (e.g., piped networks and wells) from interference, damage and destruction;

(c) Violations of the obligation to fulfil occur through the failure of States parties to take all necessary steps to ensure the realization of the right to water. Examples include, inter alia: *(i)* failure to adopt or implement a national water policy designed to ensure the right to water for everyone; *(ii)* insufficient expenditure or misallocation of public resources which results in the non-enjoyment of the right to water by individuals or groups, particularly

---

[27] See para. 23 for a definition of "third parties."

the vulnerable or marginalized; *(iii)* failure to monitor the realization of the right to water at the national level, for example by identifying right-to-water indicators and benchmarks; *(iv)* failure to take measures to reduce the inequitable distribution of water facilities and services; *(v)* failure to adopt mechanisms for emergency relief; *(vi)* failure to ensure that the minimum essential level of the right is enjoyed by everyone; *(vii)* failure of a State to take into account its international legal obligations regarding the right to water when entering into agreements with other States or with international organizations.

V. IMPLEMENTATION AT THE NATIONAL LEVEL

45. In accordance with article 2, paragraph 1, of the Covenant, States parties are required to utilize "all appropriate means, including particularly the adoption of legislative measures" in the implementation of their Covenant obligations. Every State party has a margin of discretion in assessing which measures are most suitable to meet its specific circumstances. The Covenant, however, clearly imposes a duty on each State party to take whatever steps are necessary to ensure that everyone enjoys the right to water, as soon as possible. Any national measures designed to realize the right to water should not interfere with the enjoyment of other human rights.

Legislation, strategies and policies

46. Existing legislation, strategies and policies should be reviewed to ensure that they are compatible with obligations arising from the right to water, and should be repealed, amended or changed if inconsistent with Covenant requirements.

47. The duty to take steps clearly imposes on States parties an obligation to adopt a national strategy or plan of action to realize the right to water. The strategy must: *(a)* be based upon human rights law and principles; *(b)* cover all aspects of the right to water and the corresponding obligations of States parties; *(c)* define clear objectives; *(d)* set targets or goals to be achieved and the time-frame for their achievement; *(e)* formulate adequate policies and corresponding benchmarks and indicators. The strategy should also establish institutional responsibility for the process; identify resources available to attain the objectives, targets and goals; allocate resources appropriately according to institutional responsibility; and establish accountability mechanisms to ensure the implementation of the strategy. When formulating and implementing their right to water national strategies,

States parties should avail themselves of technical assistance and cooperation of the United Nations specialized agencies (see Part VI below).

48. The formulation and implementation of national water strategies and plans of action should respect, inter alia, the principles of non-discrimination and people's participation. The right of individuals and groups to participate in decision-making processes that may affect their exercise of the right to water must be an integral part of any policy, programme or strategy concerning water. Individuals and groups should be given full and equal access to information concerning water, water services and the environment, held by public authorities or third parties.

49. The national water strategy and plan of action should also be based on the principles of accountability, transparency and independence of the judiciary, since good governance is essential to the effective implementation of all human rights, including the realization of the right to water. In order to create a favourable climate for the realization of the right, States parties should take appropriate steps to ensure that the private business sector and civil society are aware of, and consider the importance of, the right to water in pursuing their activities.

50. States parties may find it advantageous to adopt framework legislation to operationalize their right to water strategy. Such legislation should include: *(a)* targets or goals to be attained and the time-frame for their achievement; *(b)* the means by which the purpose could be achieved; *(c)* the intended collaboration with civil society, private sector and international organizations; *(d)* institutional responsibility for the process; *(e)* national mechanisms for its monitoring; and *(f)* remedies and recourse procedures.

51. Steps should be taken to ensure there is sufficient coordination between the national ministries, regional and local authorities in order to reconcile water-related policies. Where implementation of the right to water has been delegated to regional or local authorities, the State party still retains the responsibility to comply with its Covenant obligations, and therefore should ensure that these authorities have at their disposal sufficient resources to maintain and extend the necessary water services and facilities. The States parties must further ensure that such authorities do not deny access to services on a discriminatory basis.

52. States parties are obliged to monitor effectively the realization of the right to water. In monitoring progress towards the realization of the right to water, States

parties should identify the factors and difficulties affecting implementation of their obligations.

Indicators and benchmarks

53. To assist the monitoring process, right to water indicators should be identified in the national water strategies or plans of action. The indicators should be designed to monitor, at the national and international levels, the State party's obligations under articles 11, paragraph 1, and 12. Indicators should address the different components of adequate water (such as sufficiency, safety and acceptability, affordability and physical accessibility), be disaggregated by the prohibited grounds of discrimination, and cover all persons residing in the State party's territorial jurisdiction or under their control. States parties may obtain guidance on appropriate indicators from the ongoing work of the World Health Organization (WHO), the Food and Agriculture Organization of the United Nations (FAO), the United Nations Centre for Human Settlements (Habitat), the International Labour Organization (ILO), the United Nations Children's Fund (UNICEF), the United Nations Environment Programme (UNEP), the United Nations Development Programme (UNDP) and the United Nations Commission on Human Rights.

54. Having identified appropriate right to water indicators, States parties are invited to set appropriate national benchmarks in relation to each indicator.[28] During the periodic reporting procedure, the Committee will engage in a process of "scoping" with the State party. Scoping involves the joint consideration by the State party and the Committee of the indicators and national benchmarks which will then provide the targets to be achieved during the next reporting period. In the following five years, the State party will use these national benchmarks to help monitor its implementation of the right to water. Thereafter, in the subsequent reporting process, the State party and the Committee will consider whether or not the benchmarks have been achieved, and the reasons for any difficulties

---

[28] See E. Riedel, "New bearings to the State reporting procedure: practical ways to operationalize economic, social and cultural rights—The example of the right to health," in S. von Schorlemer (ed.), *Praxishandbuch UNO*, 2002, pp. 345-358. The Committee notes, for example, the commitment in the 2002 World Summit on Sustainable Development Plan of Implementation to halve, by the year 2015, the proportion of people who are unable to reach or to afford safe drinking water (as outlined in the Millennium Declaration) and the proportion of people who do not have access to basic sanitation.

that may have been encountered (see General Comment No.14 (2000), para. 58). Further, when setting benchmarks and preparing their reports, States parties should utilize the extensive information and advisory services of specialized agencies with regard to data collection and disaggregation.

Remedies and accountability

55. Any persons or groups who have been denied their right to water should have access to effective judicial or other appropriate remedies at both national and international levels (see General Comment No. 9 (1998), para. 4, and Principle 10 of the Rio Declaration on Environment and Development).[29] The Committee notes that the right has been constitutionally entrenched by a number of States and has been subject to litigation before national courts. All victims of violations of the right to water should be entitled to adequate reparation, including restitution, compensation, satisfaction or guarantees of non-repetition. National ombudsmen, human rights commissions, and similar institutions should be permitted to address violations of the right.

56. Before any action that interferes with an individual's right to water is carried out by the State party, or by any other third party, the relevant authorities must ensure that such actions are performed in a manner warranted by law, compatible with the Covenant, and that comprises: *(a)* opportunity for genuine consultation with those affected; *(b)* timely and full disclosure of information on the proposed measures; *(c)* reasonable notice of proposed actions; *(d)* legal recourse and remedies for those affected; and *(e)* legal assistance for obtaining legal remedies (see also General Comments No. 4 (1991) and No. 7 (1997)). Where such action is based on a person's failure to pay for water, their capacity to pay must be taken into account. Under no circumstances shall an individual be deprived of the minimum essential level of water.

57. The incorporation in the domestic legal order of international instruments recognizing the right to water can significantly enhance the scope and effectiveness of remedial measures and should be encouraged in all cases. Incorporation enables courts to adjudicate violations of the right to water, or at least the core obligations, by direct reference to the Covenant.

---

[29] Principle 10 of the Rio Declaration on Environment and Development (*Report of the United Nations Conference on Environment and Development,* see footnote 5 above), states with respect to environmental issues that "effective access to judicial and administrative proceedings, including remedy and redress, shall be provided."

58. Judges, adjudicators and members of the legal profession should be encouraged by States parties to pay greater attention to violations of the right to water in the exercise of their functions.

59. States parties should respect, protect, facilitate and promote the work of human rights advocates and other members of civil society with a view to assisting vulnerable or marginalized groups in the realization of their right to water.

VI. OBLIGATIONS OF ACTORS OTHER THAN STATES

60. United Nations agencies and other international organizations concerned with water, such as WHO, FAO, UNICEF, UNEP, UN-Habitat, ILO, UNDP, the International Fund for Agricultural Development (IFAD), as well as international organizations concerned with trade such as the World Trade Organization (WTO), should cooperate effectively with States parties, building on their respective expertise, in relation to the implementation of the right to water at the national level. The international financial institutions, notably the International Monetary Fund and the World Bank, should take into account the right to water in their lending policies, credit agreements, structural adjustment programmes and other development projects (see General Comment No. 2 (1990)), so that the enjoyment of the right to water is promoted. When examining the reports of States parties and their ability to meet the obligations to realize the right to water, the Committee will consider the effects of the assistance provided by all other actors. The incorporation of human rights law and principles in the programmes and policies by international organizations will greatly facilitate implementation of the right to water. The role of the International Federation of the Red Cross and Red Crescent Societies, International Committee of the Red Cross, the Office of the United Nations High Commissioner for Refugees (UNHCR), WHO and UNICEF, as well as non-governmental organizations and other associations, is of particular importance in relation to disaster relief and humanitarian assistance in times of emergencies. Priority in the provision of aid, distribution and management of water and water facilities should be given to the most vulnerable or marginalized groups of the population.

Index